Of Grasshoppers and Giants

Of Grasshoppers and Giants

A Formula for Achieving Ministers

by
Fletcher Spruce

We saw the giants . . . and we were . . . as grasshoppers.
—Num. 13:33

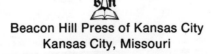
Beacon Hill Press of Kansas City
Kansas City, Missouri

Copyright, 1975
Beacon Hill Press of Kansas City

ISBN: 0-8341-0357-5

Printed in the
United States of America

Dedication

To the men
who proclaim
the
Holy Ought
in
an age of
unholy opportunities

CONTENTS

Foreword   8

Preface   9

By Way of Explanation   11

PART ONE—GOD'S PATTERN FOR
SUCCESSFUL MINISTERS
Then thou shalt have good success
(Josh. 1:8).

1. The Ministerial Success Syndrome   13
2. Frankness About Frustrations   19
3. Characteristics of Effective Ministers   28
4. A Sanctified Self-image   35
5. Good Grooming for God's Man   41
6. The Menace of Mediocrity   49
7. A Sense of Strategy   58
8. Techniques of Anticipation   65
9. The Minister as Executive   73

PART TWO—THE FINE ART OF
DEVELOPING LAY LEADERSHIP
*Provide . . . able men . . . and place such
over them, to be rulers* (Exod. 18:21).

10. Men of Distinction   84
11. Concepts for Spiritual Leaders   88
12. Search for Excellence   92
13. How Leadership Shows Through   96
14. Tools for Problem Solvers   100
15. Profile of a Troubleshooter   103
16. On Learning to Cope with Problems   111
17. How to Pick a Winner   116

PART THREE—THE POSTURE OF
AN ACHIEVER

I can do all things through Christ which strengtheneth me (Phil. 4:13).

18. The Grasshopper Complex   121
19. The Sleeping Sickness of Status Quoism   126
20. Games Failures Play   130
21. Twelve Keys to Proficiency   135
22. Brother Ho-hum Comes Alive   140
23. How to Sustain Motivation   146
24. Preparing Yourself for Action   152
25. Preparing Your People for Action   155

Reference Notes   159

Foreword

Regarding Forewords, a famous Bible scholar once said that good books don't need them and bad books don't deserve them. Well, this is one book that really does not need a foreword. But Dr. Fletcher Spruce asked me to provide a foreword for this book. And then he slipped away suddenly just before the manuscript was finished.

But really Fletcher Spruce is not dead. He just waved good-bye and took an early flight to the Eternal City. As long as people read *Standard,* they will think again and again of the warm and interesting articles that Fletcher Spruce contributed for so many years. We will also recall the sharp point that often penetrated deeply into our consciousness and punctured some balloons we had loved too long.

It is thus with this book. *Of Grasshoppers and Giants* speaks to an audience that Fletcher Spruce knew well and loved very deeply—the ministry. Even a casual reading will bring the reader into a firm grasp of self-appraisal. It may be attitudes, perhaps a sense of inefficiency, perhaps poor motivation. But whatever it be, a reading of this book will point out and analyze the weak links. And what's more, there will be more than ministerial diagnosis; there will be prescription for ministerial improvement. And let the reader recall that the author knew many fruitful years as a pastor and district superintendent.

So read *Of Grasshoppers and Giants* and be the better —much better.

—Norman R. Oke

Preface

1. This book is not for everybody. Some laymen are already alive, already motivating others, and already achieving for God in their churches and in their communities. So they do not need this book. Some ministers, too, are already holy achievers and are getting worthy results for God and for their churches. They do not need this book either.

2. But this book is for somebody. It may be for you. It is for many of God's good, yet sterile, saints—unproductive as far as spiritual results are concerned. This book is for the layman who is disturbed about the level of results he is seeing in his own life and in the lives of other laymen in his church.

This book is for the preacher who is preaching the same sermons he preached 10 years ago, whose altars are mostly barren, whose church membership rolls show about as many members dropped as added by profession of faith, whose total ministry is making little impact in the local church or in the community. This book is also for the minister who down deep on the inside is desperate about empty benches, is frustrated about fruitless altar calls, is hungry for genuine revival in his church, is vitally concerned about involving laymen in the leadership of his church, and is reaching out for something to make his church grow.

3. This book does not offer a cure-all for church problems. It is not a magic wand which may be waved across the pulpit and the congregation to produce remarkable results. It suggests no easy methods either, whereby everyone can think positively and reduce all the problems to the minimum.

4. This book is a heart cry from the author to preachers and laymen everywhere who are seeking to be more

productive in God's work. Obviously, the beginning place is the prayer closet, the practice of fasting and waiting on God, the anointing of the Spirit upon lives of preacher and layman alike. There can be no substitute for this. However, spirituality alone, though it is the starting point and foundation, is not enough.

5. This book is an appeal for right practices, current methods and motivational procedures beyond the altar. It is never enough to just be spiritual. Beyond good religion is needed common sense, hard work, organizational ability, leadership programming, executive methods, proper attitudes, up-to-date procedures, and the faith which produces spiritual results.

6. This book could be dangerous. If you do not believe in a successful, spiritual ministry in your church; if you do not believe that your church is able to grow and must grow; if you do not believe that your church can be both a growing church and a spiritual church without compromise, then this book could be dangerous to your faith and to your practice. This book could be dangerous also if you believe that the things espoused herein are so but do not apply to you; that they apply only to the Baptists or to the Presbyterians, not to your humble group. This book could be dangerous if you believe God wants your church to be small so that it can be clean. This book could be dangerous if you believe that people are turned off by rugged standards and by solid holiness preaching.

7. This book may be helpful to some who read it. If one person is inspired to greater things for Christ and His Church; if one person is motivated to win more souls to the Master in these last days; if one person gets excited about making his church larger, then "to God be the glory." Amen!

—FLETCHER SPRUCE

By Way of Explanation

My father completed the bulk of this manuscript prior to his death at Christmastime, 1974. All but two chapters (9 and 15) were typed in their first draft, and only the final editing needed to be completed. Together we frequently discussed the need for such a work, particularly for young men entering the pastoral ministry. Even in the press of his other numerous duties, our family encouraged him to continue this monumental effort. In the providence of God, he was given nearly six months of recuperation time immediately following open-heart surgery in 1973 to complete the research and begin writing. For him, writing was a joy, not a job. And in that spirit he was able to author this, his last work, before resuming normal activities.

He had expressed to us his appreciation of Miss Londa Fausz for typing large portions from dictation. Since it became my responsibility to complete the work from her typing, I join my father in his gratitude. Mrs. Stephen Collins, of Champaign First Church of the Nazarene, typed the entire manuscript in its completed form, and for her effort I offer my sincere appreciation.

Members of the Book Committee of the church have been a source of encouragement to me. For nearly as long as I can remember, I know that their fellowship and partnership with my father had been a well of perpetual trust and love.

I remember hearing his voice 30 years ago in family prayer. And the last time we were together as a family, he led us in prayer. He was a man *of* the Word. He was able to minister because he was ministered unto. It is the prayer of his immediate family that this volume will enable the pastor and his people to more adequately pursue their ministry in optimism, devotion, and love.

—JAMES R. SPRUCE
Champaign, Ill.

PART ONE

GOD'S PATTERN FOR SUCCESSFUL MINISTERS

Then thou shalt have good success.
—JOSH. 1:8

Chapter 1

THE MINISTERIAL SUCCESS SYNDROME

Billy Graham relates an incident that happened during a New York City crusade in Madison Square Garden. Many hours had been spent in prayer and many months in preparation. But the team was greatly concerned about the atmosphere of apprehension and questioning regarding the massive spiritual enterprise. There were gigantic spiritual barriers. Then on the opening night Dr. Graham and his team met for prayer and last-minute planning in an anteroom, concerned about the first service of that heavy undertaking. No one was smiling.

Soon the door burst open and Ethel Waters confidently walked into the room. Seeing the distress and apparent lack of confidence that etched the faces of all present, she inquired as to the nature of the problem and received an immediate reply from several members of the team. Then, as only Ethel Waters can do, she said, "Look here, children. God don't deal in no flops!"

Is Failure a Mark of Spirituality?

A man once testified in prayer meeting: "I would rather be a failure for God than a success for the devil." The last part of the statement sounds fine. No one wants to be a success for the devil. But on the other hand, should any Christian be willing to be a failure for God? One of the songs we used to sing had a line in it that went something like this:

O to be nothing, nothing . . .

In its context the thought is one of complete consecration. But there is danger if (as did the Sunday school lad) we sing it:

*O to **do** nothing, nothing . . .*

Should a minister be content to fail if God wills it? Should a Christian worker be content to fail if God wills it? Or perhaps the better question is: *"Does* God will it?" Is failure an evidence of spirituality? It is not easy to get away from Ethel Waters' classic thesis: "God don't deal in no flops." Or in the words of another: "I would rather attempt to do great things and fail, than to attempt nothing and succeed." Rudyard Kipling expressed it this way: "We have 40 million reasons for failure, but not a single excuse."

Is the Desire for Success in God's Work Sinful?

Is it wrong for a pastor to strive to be a successful pastor? Is it sinful for a Sunday school teacher to want to be a successful Sunday school teacher? Should a man of God have an ambition to win many souls and see the church grow? What goals are worthy for a consecrated layman? When Albert Einstein said, "Try not to become a man of success but rather try to become a man of value," was he downgrading quantity and upgrading quality—or both? Is it possible to be a man of value without being a man of success? Contrariwise, is it possible to be a man of success without being a man of value? Somerset Maugham answers this way: "The common idea that success spoils people by making them vain, egotistic, and self-com-

14

placent is erroneous; on the contrary, it makes them, for the most part, humble, tolerant, and kind. Failure makes people cruel and bitter."[1]

What Is Success in God's Work?

In a study of the top executives in 500 of our largest corporations, we find a profile of a successful man. Here is a part of that profile:

He is 53 years old.

He has a graduate degree.

He has held his present position five years.

He works 50 to 60 hours per week.

His salary is $100,000 per year.

Earl Nightingale has defined success as the progressive realization of a worthy goal. W. H. Belk, Jr., of the Belk Stores, observed: "There is nothing noble in being superior to some other man. True nobility is in being superior to your previous self."[2] Another has indicated that success is like a pair of shoes; the same size does not fit everyone.

Lawrence Welk has this to say about the nature of success:

> Success is probably one of the most common of the goals of men . . . yet seldom does a man attempt clearly to define for himself exactly what it is. We all want it, yet few of us know exactly what we want. . . . Can a person be considered successful no matter what his accomplishments are, if he is spiritually barren, emotionally unstable, or intellectually sterile? Is he successful if he is socially misplaced, or if his family is unhappy? Is he successful if he lives only for himself and his own selfish gains and advancement? Is the sole yardstick of success such a thing as power, prestige, influence, standing in the community, education, or for that matter, a combination of all of these? No, it is not, for even with these there could be misery, unhappiness,

15

moral corruption and ineffectiveness. As far as I know
there is only one way of defining and measuring success. It is in doing one's best to make the most of one's
self.[3]

Success ought not to be measured by what a man has but
by what a man is doing with what he has. It is relative.
It does not mean that a man has progressed to the limit of
his capabilities, but that he is surely and steadily making
remarkable progress in that direction. It is not in the winning triumph but in the constant struggle that success
blossoms beautifully.

Addressing a missionary convention in Indiana, Elmer
Schmelzenbach said of his father, a pioneer to the Swazis:

In those beginning days, twice they burned the hut
he built to shelter his family. Two years he labored without one convert. Today we have 22,000 church members
and an average of 53,000 per Sunday in Sunday school
in our churches and preaching points in South Africa.

It is well that we remind ourselves that there are many
kinds of success. And perhaps the greatest of all is the
success of the spirit that keeps itself undefeated and
aspiring whether we are happy or unhappy, famous or
unknown, rich or poor, successful or unsuccessful—and
whether life is rewarding or bitter.

It is a mistake to think of success as something one
gets. Rather it is something a man is—and does. Successful lives are built by successful men, and successful enter-
prises are but the projection of successful men. The visible
success proves that an invisible something has happened
inside the man. He has refused to accept mediocrity and
has risen above it. He is making the most of his total self:
body, mind, and spirit.

The Success-Failure Complex

I have before me a four-cartoon strip of *Peanuts* by
Schulz. Charlie Brown is dressed in a baseball suit and

cap, dragging bat and glove in a very dejected manner. And here is what he is saying in the four pictures:

Good grief!
One hundred and eighty-four to nothing!
I don't understand it . . .
How can we lose when we are so sincere?

Charlie Brown lost the game—disastrously—even though he was sincere! And I have known some very sincere (and spiritual) preachers (and laymen) who were miserable failures in the work of the Lord. Why do so many churches level off and quit growing by the time they reach a membership of 100 or 500 or 1,000?

I have before me statistics of two churches in the same metropolitan area. Both have been through relocation programs and have adequate buildings, finances, and leadership. One of these churches spurted up to an average attendance of 300 and leveled off. Now, after almost 30 years, that church is running just below that figure. The other church did not have a spurt but a slowly rising tide. Its modest but steady growth through these 30 years still continues, and it is a spiritual powerhouse in the community. Why did one church quit growing 30 years ago? Why did the other keep growing? And what about the church you attend? How much has it increased in the past 5 years? 10 years? 30 years?

After giving a performance, an outstanding woman pianist was having coffee with a group of ladies. One of the women said to her: "I'd give anything to be able to play as you do."

To this the pianist replied: "Oh, no, you wouldn't. If you *would,* you could play as well as, or perhaps better than, I. You would give anything to be able to play as well as I except the time and the hard work—the two things it takes. You would not sit and practice, hour after hour, day after day, year after year." Blunt words, but true.

Would you give *anything* to see your church succeed at the business of winning men and women to Christ? Failure in God's work is not a sign of spirituality—it is sinful! The desire for success in God's work is not sinful—the lack of it is.

Let us pay attention to a prayer by Peter Marshall:

O God, our Father, let us not be content to wait and see what will happen, but give us the determination to make the right things happen. While time is running out, save us from the patience that is akin to cowardice. Give us the courage to be either hot or cold, to stand for something, lest we fall for anything. In Jesus' name. Amen.[4]

Churches do not stagnate—but sometimes people do.
Altars are not barren—but sometimes people are.
Sermons do not go flat—but sometimes preachers do.
Communities do not become gospel-hardened—but sometimes church members do.
God does not fail—but sometimes we do.
So . . .
Churches come alive when people come alive.
Altars are fruitful when people are fruitful.
Sermons are powerful when preachers are powerful.
Communities respond when church members respond.
God's work succeeds when God's workers succeed.

Chapter 2

FRANKNESS
ABOUT FRUSTRATIONS

From a recent church bulletin comes this interesting quoted paragraph:

> Have you ever tried preaching 156 sermons each year to the same people? Have you ever tried to get along with 200 people and yet please the Lord? Have you ever pondered over a way to motivate people to attend every service? Have you ever spent hours in prayer and preparation and feel that very little was accomplished? Did you ever try to bind up a broken heart or reestablish a broken home? Did you ever pour out energy to convert a soul and get no response? Did you ever try to lead, and discover that few would follow your leadership? If not, you cannot know what it means to be a pastor!

Because of the nature of his work, the minister finds that college and seminary training cannot adequately inform him of the frustrations he is to face. Experience is the best—and almost the only—teacher in this regard. Let us take a look at a few of these frustrations with frankness and try to find some constructive answers. Let us begin with

10 Pressure Points on Preachers

1. Personal Pressure. Am I called? Am I spiritual? Am I succeeding? Will my health fail? What if . . . ?

2. *Family Pressure.* How can I find more time to spend with my family? Is it right to neglect my children when they need a father very much? How can I help my wife through this time of illness? How can our family become more united?

3. *Financial Pressure.* Where, on my salary, can I get money for clothes, furniture, food, automobile, books, medical expenses, education of our children, future security, and a thousand other things? Shall I moonlight? Shall I ask my wife to help me make a living and hire a baby-sitter—or *be* the baby-sitter?

4. *Results Pressure.* Our church *must* have a revival if I am to remain here. How can I get the church to grow? How can I reach my personal goals and the goals of the church? How can we ever get that building program going? What can I do to get our people to tithe? To give beyond the tithe?

5. *Priorities Pressure.* There is too much to do—and not enough time to get it all done. How can I get others to help me do the work that laymen ought to be doing? What can I leave undone?

6. *Church Board Pressure.* How can I get the board members to pull together? What can I do to get them off dead center? How can I keep them from going off on tangents and neglecting vital issues? How can I motivate them?

7. *Difficult Saints Pressure.* How can I handle Mr. Big? What can be done to overcome conflicts among my members? How can I get rid of their negativism? How can I defuse their negative attitudes toward me?

8. *Headquarters Pressure.* How can we pay all these big budgets? How can we possibly meet all those high goals set by headquarters and the district superintendent? Look at all those special offerings! And those detailed reports!

9. *Ministerial Brethren Pressure.* They keep asking

me how many I had in Sunday school last Sunday! How many came to the altar? They keep bragging about their trips to the Holy Land. And I never get the promotions others get!

10. *Divine Pressure.* Have I failed God someplace? Why do my prayers go unanswered? Does God expect me to do more than I am doing?

It all reminds us of a telegram sent by General William Booth to the Salvation Army lass, Mary Ann Parkin: "Proceed to your assignment at King's Lynn. No home. No hall. No friends. No money. You must succeed."

The Overemployed Pastor

In January, 1972, I conducted a survey of the opinions of church board members on the Northeastern Indiana District regarding what they thought about their pastor's work habits, use of time, his talents, etc. On the question: "How much time do you think the pastor should devote to . . ." (such areas as calling, praying, sermon preparation, reading, manual labor on the church buildings, etc.), we discovered that, in one case, the total was 198 hours per week! Several thought the pastor should work more than the 168 hours in the week. The average expectation of their pastor was about 80 hours per week—around 12 hours per day 7 days per week! How many hours should a pastor work each day to do justice to his work? Let us consider a

10-Point Job Description for the Pastor

1. *Personal Devotions.* He must (like any spiritual person) devote time to the cultivation of his own spiritual life by Bible reading and prayer.

2. *Sermon Preparation.* It has been said that an hour's preparation should be spent for each minute of the sermon's duration!

3. Reading. Preachers ought to read a book (100 pages) each day, five days each week. Included here is the reading for sermon preparation and devotions.

4. Pastoral Calling. Hospital calls, calls in homes of members and prospects, absentee visitation, community surveys, soul winning visits. One thousand per year?

5. Organization and Administration. Included here are all the hours spent in perfecting and improving the function of all areas and departments.

6. Promotion and Programming. Campaigns, planning, goal setting with various groups, as well as methods for growth are included here.

7. Finances. The pastor helps in projecting annual budgets for operation and in devising ways and means to help the church meet these responsibilities.

8. Counselling. The minister must help people cope with all sorts of problems and guide them to scriptural solutions and spiritual victories.

9. Outside Interests. These include community responsibilities beyond the local church as well as denominational concerns of the zone, district, and general church.

10. Lay Responsibilities. Often the pastor is called upon to do secretarial work, bulletin preparation and mailing, record keeping, and even (in extreme cases) custodial services—all of which ought to be delegated to others.

We are reminded at this point of the new salesman who, having completed all his training and motivation classes, was sent out to sell his company's product. At the end of the day he returned, somewhat downcast. When the supervisor asked him if he got any orders, he said: "Yes! I called all day and got two orders: 'Get out!' and 'Stay out!'"

The Underemployed Laymen

The wife of one of our fine board members was not well and I had come for a brief visit and prayer in the home, just one block from the church I was pastoring in a southern city. I had concluded my visit and prayer, and the husband was walking to the door with me when he said (a bit sharply, I thought), "Come back in about six months. Our former pastor used to come every Tuesday and spend the afternoon with us."

"I will be back before midnight if you need me," I replied as calmly as I could. "Otherwise, I will be out calling on the unsaved in the community. Maybe you can join me when your wife gets to feeling better. You see, I have about 600 people to look after."

As was my practice, the first few months in that pastorate I had called in the home of each church member. I then began a door-to-door survey of each home within a mile of the church. When I knocked on the door of the house adjoining the property of this fine board member, I found a splendid unchurched family who were responsive. When I told them that their nearest neighbor was a member of our church board, the husband replied: "I have lived here six years and he has never mentioned the church to me." The four members of this new family came to church the next Sunday, were converted within a few weeks, started tithing, joined the church, and became faithful members.

Let's face it! The church is a giant—a sleeping giant! The laity is largely asleep in the grandstands and the clergy is largely drugged—overwhelmed on the field of action. Our approach is the reverse of the New Testament pattern. We have seated the players in the grandstands and have sent the coach out on the field of action to face the enemy—almost single-handed. Could this be a prime factor in the unbelievable inertia that plagues so many congregations today? Someone has expressed it in a church bulletin in these words (and some of my own) by listing "12 Problems in the Church":

1. The unread Book
2. The unbended knee
3. The unpaid tithe
4. The unspiritual "saint"
5. The unattended church
6. The underpaid pastor
7. The unfaithful leaders
8. The uninteresting teachers
9. The uncompassionate heart
10. The undisturbed sinner
11. The unconcern for the lost
12. The unrealized cross of Christ

28 Temptations Preachers Face

Let us sketch quickly some of the many unique temptations faced by the minister—all of which add to his several areas of frustration:

Occupational Temptations

1. Preaching—sermonettes or sermon monsters?
2. Studying—bookishness or booklessness?
3. Calling—300 pastoral visits annually, or 3,000?
4. Accomplishing—souls being added, edified, harnessed?

Temperamental Temptations

5. Recline—Why work so hard and long in this rat race?
6. Whine—Why don't they appreciate me and promote me?
7. Dine—Wonder who will invite us to dinner today?

24

8. Shine—This sermon (or song) should bring a great response!

Psychological Temptations
9. Alibiing—No other preacher has made this go, either.
10. Fussing—I never saw so much hard-core opposition in my life.
11. Gliding—If they don't make calls, I will not make them either.
12. Procrastinating—Let's put off that revival another year.

Philosophical Temptations
13. Negativism—It just cannot be done in this wicked town.
14. Legalism—If they don't dress like I do, I'll skin them alive.
15. Professionalism—I am called to preach, not to build the church.
16. Status Quoism—if we can just hold our own, that's good enough.

Personality Temptations
17. Kick-back—If they buck me, I'll turn them out of the church.
18. Break-easy—I simply refuse to put up with opposition.
19. Lone-wolf—I'd rather watch TV than go to the zone rally.
20. Know-it-all—You are wrong if you disagree with me.

Dispositional Temptations
21. Promotion—I'm tired of all this junk mail from headquarters.
22. Loyalty—It doesn't worry me if I can't pay all those big budgets.

23. Details—Why should I send in all those reports?

24. Work—Forty hours per week is more than they pay me for.

Domestic Temptations

25. House—Lawn mowed? Porch clean? Backyard free from litter?

26. Home—Family altar? Time with my family? Happiness?

27. Hobbies—Am I taking a day off each week?

28. Money—Do I have a weekly, workable family budget?

The Buck Stops Here

President Truman had a motto on his desk which read: "The Buck Stops Here." In a very real sense this is true of the pastor also, for every pastor has about the kind of church he wants—or the kind he is willing to put up with. The final responsibility rests with him. The pastor determines the level of effectiveness of his ministry. The church board is not altogether responsible for what happens in the church, for these people are part-time, off-hours leaders. Their full-time job interest is elsewhere and they cannot be expected to give full-time service to the church as does the pastor. Therefore the pastor is the executive, the manager of the church—full-time, not part-time. He is a specialist.

Here is a partial list of

15 Pastoral Responsibilities

1. The pastor is the chairman of the church board.

2. The pastor is president of the church in meetings involving official business.

3. The pastor is head of all auxiliaries, departments, committees.

4. The pastor is responsible for nominations, elections, appointments.

5. The pastor is responsible for the total financial picture of the church.

6. The pastor is responsible for the church and Sunday school membership rolls.

7. The pastor is responsible for programming and promotion in all areas.

8. The pastor is responsible for the quality of teaching and training.

9. The pastor is responsible for the evangelistic thrust of the church.

10. The pastor is responsible for the doctrinal soundness of his people.

11. The pastor is responsible for the atmosphere of the services.

12. The pastor is responsible for the physical equipment of the church.

13. The pastor is responsible for the cultural and social tone of the church.

14. The pastor is responsible for the morale of the people.

15. The pastor is responsible for the spiritual condition of the people.

These are some of the problems and frustrations in running a church. But we have only skimmed the surface. Nor have we offered solutions. The finding of these solutions will be the purpose of the balance of this book.

Chapter 3

CHARACTERISTICS OF EFFECTIVE MINISTERS

In making pastoral arrangements it has been my observation that members of church boards are more selective now than ever as they interview prospective pastors to recommend to the congregation. Not many years ago the board would accept the recommendation of the district superintendent and the congregation would concur with a yes vote. In more recent times, however, the board members are not only asking questions, they are interviewing prospective pastors and their wives—often at length—and usually with satisfying results. In setting up these interviews, I have discovered that church board members usually ask about the same questions before they invite a man for the interview. Here are

14 Questions Most Often Asked About Ministers:

1. Is he a spiritual man—holy in all aspects of his life?

2. Does he get along well in the area of human relations?

3. Can he preach? Does he study? Are his sermons fresh, forceful, relevant?

4. Do the churches he pastors enjoy growth under his leadership?

5. Is he able to lead the congregation in areas of finance?

6. Does he have a good record of paying all his budgets?

7. Is he a hard worker in areas of calling and witnessing?

8. Does he display effective leadership and administration?

9. Does he get people saved and get them to join the church?

10. Does he build new Christians into solid churchmen?

11. Does he cooperate with the district and general program?

12. Does he keep the standards without being fanatical?

13. Does he build ahead for revivals and evangelism in the church?

14. Tell us about his wife and children.

In the early chapters of the Book of Joshua is recorded the story of one of God's most able achievers. Joshua was to succeed where Moses failed. How did he do it? Here are shown

10 Characteristics of Effective Ministers

1. He Heard a Call and Could Not Hush It

"The Lord spake unto Joshua . . . saying, . . . arise, go over this Jordan, thou, and all this people" (1:1-2). It was the Lord who called and Joshua kept that call clear. He did not dodge it—nor silence it. He simply obeyed, and the call became the motivating force in all his future life. His was a divine assignment and there was no sidestepping—no turning back. His faithfulness to God's call proved his consecration. Effective ministers keep the call clear, always.

When William E. Sangster was given a large responsibility of leadership in English Methodism, he wrote:

> This is the will of God for me. I did not choose it. I sought to escape from it. But it has come.
>
> Something else has come too. A sense of certainty that God does not want me only for a preacher. He wants me also for a leader . . .
>
> I feel a commissioning to work under God for the revival of this branch of His church—careless of my own reputation; indifferent to the comments of older and jealous men. I am thirty-six.
>
> If I am to serve God in this way, I must no longer shrink from the task, but *do* it.
>
> I have examined my heart for ambition. I am certain it is not there. . . . By the will of God, this is my task. God help me.[1]

2. *He Had a Goal, and Kept His Eye on It*

That goal was Canaan Land and the conquest of this territory for God. "Every place that the sole of your foot shall tread upon, that have I given unto you" (1:3). Without a goal he might have ended up in Babylon or the Red Sea. But he got his goal from God and the vision never dimmed. Blessed is the preacher with some goals! How many new converts do you plan to win this year? How many new members by profession of faith? How many calls do you plan to make this year? How many books do you plan to read this week? What are your planned increases in Sunday school average attendance? What is the total projected budget of your church for the next year? How do you plan to raise this money? What is your preaching program for the next 12 months? Achievers set goals to go by.

3. *He Had a Program and Put It into Action*

"Joshua . . . sent . . . two men to spy secretly, saying,

Go view the land" (2:1). He had a plan—a program to help him reach his goal. Goals alone are not enough. The man who is not planning to succeed is planning to fail. Effective ministers plan to be effective. Successful ministers pay adequate attention to programming. Ruth Lommantzsch has said it well:

Tomorrow's achievements, be whatever they may,
Are the future results of good planning today.

4. He Had Some Priorities and Kept Them in Perspective

"Turn not from it to the right hand or to the left" (1:7). Are there so many things to be done that you are spreading yourself over too many jobs—and doing justice to none of them? Two things will help you: (1) Delegate some of your responsibilities to others, and (2) set some priorities for yourself.

The story is told that Charles Schwab had a problem at this point and called in a specialist to help him. The specialist gave Mr. Schwab four simple steps to take:

1. Make a list of the six most important things you must do tomorrow.
2. Now rank these six in the order of their importance.
3. Now do the first thing first. Stay with it until you finish it. Then go to the second, and stay with it until you finish it. Then to the third.
4. Don't worry if you fail to finish the list. You are doing the most important things first. Do this every day and you will succeed.

By following these simple rules Mr. Schwab was able to build a $100 million steel industry. Any minister will do more by sticking to his priorities than he would do if he had no priorities.

5. He Was Assigned a Place of Leadership and Accepted the Challenge

"Then Joshua commanded the officers of the people" (1:10). Leadership is thrust upon the shoulders of a God-called man whether he relishes it or not. It is an integral part of his calling and there is no escaping from it. Joshua was neither a dictator nor a pushover. His tongue was not sharp like the crack of a whip, nor was it as "smooth as butter." He disciplined and motivated himself that he might be a worthy leader of others. By organizing himself and his work, he was able to organize others. An unknown poet penned this bit of doggerel:

> *I nibble at this, I nibble at that,*
> *But I never finish what I am at;*
> *I work as hard as anyone,*
> *And yet I get so little done;*
> *I'd do so much you'd be surprised*
> *If I could just get myself organized.*

6. He Had Some Friends and Gave Them a Holy Challenge

"Sanctify yourselves: for to morrow the Lord will do wonders among you" (3:5). He discovered that people are best motivated by a holy challenge. They are never adequately motivated by such negative exhortations as: "Now let's all go out and make those calls this week" or "We just must pay all these big budgets, so let's all double-tithe today." Joshua did it by saying, "To morrow the Lord will do wonders among you." Then the people began to look up with expectancy and hope—and followed him because he gave them something to believe in, and Someone to help them.

7. He Was Not Afraid of Hard Work

"And Joshua rose early in the morning" (3:1). It was not his practice to watch the "late-late" on television and then sleep in until 8:30 a.m. He had more important things to do, like planning and working and praying and programming. It was no small job to organize a million or so ex-slaves for a relocation program across a bridgeless Jordan

32

into hostile territory. If anyone has any more hard work and exacting demands thrust upon him than a dedicated minister of the gospel, I have not met him. And while no work is more demanding, no work is more rewarding. Laymen should not pity him; they should join hands with him in this ripe harvest, for it is their harvest, too! This little verse by an unknown author says it well:

> *Better try to do something*
> *And fail in the deed—*
> *Than to try to do nothing*
> *And always succeed.*

8. He Had a Failure and the Courage to Reverse It

Moses and Caleb and Joshua had tasted the bitter dregs of defeat 40 years before, as recorded in Numbers 13 and 14. Caleb and Joshua agreed that with God victory was assured, but the other 10 spies were filled with fear, saying, "We saw the giants . . . and we were in our own sight as grasshoppers" (13:33). Despair filled the air and the doubters prevailed, and "all the congregation bade stone them with stones" (14:10). So they delayed their conquest of Canaan 40 years.

Joshua never forgot this setback. But instead of allowing it to embitter him, it enriched him, challenged him, and put fiber into his soul and courage into his heart. Failure has a way of making some people bitter and others better. God uses the man who knows how to make stepping-stones of his failures.

9. He Had a Jordan and Got His Feet Wet in It

"As soon as the soles of the feet . . . shall rest in the waters . . . the waters shall stand upon an heap" (3:13). Joshua was not to speak to the water nor to strike the water to make it divide, as did Moses at the Red Sea. The people were simply to start walking into the water and to expect it to divide before them—because God said it would

33

happen. It was to be a step of faith! And the waters did part!

There are times when preachers must get their feet wet—not in foolhardy excursions, but in clear, calm obedience to God's guidance, leaving the results with Him. Faith that gets results is more than mere believing. It is acting on that which we believe. And that action often calls for courage as shown by these lines of Charles Buxton Going: "The longer I live the more deeply I am convinced that that which makes the difference between one man and another—between the weak and the powerful, the great and the insignificant, is energy—invincible determination—a purpose once formed, then death or victory."[2]

10. He Had a Presence and the Enemy Could Not Resist Him

"We have heard how the Lord dried up the water of the Red Sea . . . and . . . our hearts did melt" (2:10-11). Here is the ultimate secret of Joshua's effectiveness: the Presence! This is what gave him courage and the enemy terror. God's presence is the secret Weapon in every battle, the unexplainable Factor in all our holy endeavors. Our best hope is not in training, equipment, planning, buildings, personnel, and programming—important as all these factors are. The Presence is our hope! The preacher who would be effective begins at this point and keeps this point in proper perspective at all times. John Wesley said, "Give me one hundred men who fear nothing but sin and desire nothing but God, and I care not a straw if they be clergymen or laymen; such alone will shake the gates of hell and set up the kingdom of heaven on earth."

34

Chapter 4

A SANCTIFIED SELF-IMAGE

Every minister ought to try to crawl outside and take a look at himself once in a while. And he ought to respect, and be alert to, the evaluation of his associates.

Why? What difference does it make what a man thinks of himself? Plenty! The children of Israel said, "We were in our own sight as grasshoppers" (Num. 13:33). But not Nehemiah. He said: "I am doing a great work, so that I cannot come down" (Neh. 6:3). That image of himself and his work sustained him under pressure and saved him from defeat. Solomon wrote, "As he thinketh in his heart, so is he" (Prov. 23:7), revealing that man makes his thoughts and the thoughts make the man. Paul put it this way: "I can do all things through Christ which strengtheneth me" (Phil. 4:13)—indicating the secret of his success. Jesus said to the father of an afflicted child: "If thou canst believe, all things are possible" (Mark 9:23), showing the close ties between a man's self-image and his faith for accomplishment.

The study of self-image psychology is as old as the Judeo-Christian teachings of God's Word. Only now in recent times we have clothed it in new concepts and modern terminology.

Someone has observed that back of every light that

floods the room with brightness is a powerhouse that generates the current. Just so, back of every personality that spreads brightness and goodness is a powerhouse of right thinking and worthwhile purpose. The kind of man God uses is the man who is aware that he is a child of the King. What does this involve?

Self-confidence

A sanctified self-image involves self-confidence. Samuel Johnson reminds us that self-confidence is the first requisite to a great undertaking. At this point let us make a clear distinction between self-confidence and humility. Occasionally a spiritual person will take the I-am-nothing attitude. But this is hardly harmonious with the I-am-a-child-of-the-King concept. If a person is truly a child of the King, he is a somebody and not a nobody. He is a God-made man who is stamped with the image of the King.

This makes no allowance for the braggart—the swaggering cock-of-the-walk. Nor does it allow for the weak-worm-of-the-dust-type personality. It simply brings a man to say to himself: "I am God's man, called to do God's work in God's time and in God's place. I will be faithful and God and I together will achieve great things for His glory."

Self-confidence involves self-forgiveness. It involves self-respect. It involves self-awareness. And it involves a larger confidence in God who is able to make us more than conquerors in every situation.

Self-discipline

A sanctified self-image also calls for a sanctified self-discipline. Paul said, "I keep under my body, and bring it into subjection: lest . . . I myself should be a castaway" (1 Cor. 9:27). Phillips translates it this way: "I am my body's sternest master, for fear . . . I should myself be disqualified." In *Wake Up and Live,* Dorothea Brande gives us several "Disciplines of Life" to which I have added some of my own: silence, concentration, writing, speech, decisions, time, eating, working, playing, study, emotions, planning.[1]

A disciplined man is a strong man. An undisciplined man is a weak man. The effective person puts aside some things that are desirable that he may discipline himself into the finest activity that God has for him: winning souls and building the kingdom of God.

Live as if you were the person you ought to be! Set some long-range goals and break them up into daily bite-sized goals—into weekly and monthly and yearly chunks. Then chew on them and digest them! Avoid the vocabulary of moribund, negative defeatism. Talk successfully. Preach from a positive viewpoint that motivates, challenges, inspires, and generates self-confidence in your people. Down with the grasshopper complex! Up with a handful of faith-challenges Jesus left for you!

Self-motivation

A sanctified self-image demands a sanctified self-motivation. Since the preacher does not punch a time clock, nor is he allowed the luxury of quitting when the whistle blows, he must have his own self-starter in working order every morning and he must have the stamina to keep himself going every evening. His highest motivation is the call of God burning in his own soul at all times.

The leader must be a self-starter before he can start other people. The secret is in the man himself—not in God alone—not in the people—not in the circumstances—not in the program. U. S. Andersen reminds us:

> The power of thought is that it can move you, not the world. The usefulness of thought is that it trains

you, not someone else. If you train yourself to sit there, that's just what you do. . . . Are the things you're thinking training you to take right action?[2]

Self-direction

A sanctified self-image implies a sanctified self-direction. If motivation sets a man in motion, self-direction determines where that man will go and what he will accomplish. Isaiah, pointing to Christ, says: "I set my face like a flint" (50:7). Paul said, "I must by all means keep this feast" (Acts 18:21); and again: "I appeal to Caesar" (25:11). In each of these cases we see self-direction demonstrated. These people knew where they were going and they knew what they wanted to do. Self-direction involves self-decision. Quoting again from Mr. Andersen:

> What a limiting legacy Sigmund Freud left us when he told us that we are what our past has made us. Millions of people are walking around today with the idea that they can't do a thing about their lives because the past has trapped them where they are. They discount the greatest power of their own minds . . . which can sever them from the past anytime they are willing to discipline toward growth.[3]

Self-sustenance

A sanctified self-image has a self-sustaining power. Some people have self-confidence and self-motivation and even self-direction, but they do not have staying power—they do not sustain themselves in the long pull. Their spirits sag when the going gets rough. They fail when they see the rocky path to the high peak. They faint and quit when the work is hard. But God's achiever is the man who keeps himself going beyond the glamor of the beginning.

Of course it is a rat race! Certainly there are tensions and pressures and deadlines and reports—and laymen who would rather be left in their narrow ruts than be motivated! But you will never be the person you ought to be if the pressure and the tension and the self-discipline were taken out of your life!

Is a minister backslidden simply because he does not possess these qualities? Because he has bumped a brick wall that will not crack? Because he is about to question his ability to fulfill his calling in a worthy way? Because he must go to another church and there is no other church open? Because some say he has failed when he knows he has done his best under God?

No! A thousand times NO! And don't you believe it! Every man has his caves and his juniper trees in due season!

But *faith* is the key! Faith in yourself—your work—your God! The foundation of our faith is the point at which the devil can get in his most telling licks. If Satan can get you to look upon yourself as a grasshopper, then he knows other people will look upon you in the same manner. But Paul found a better way: "I can do all things through Christ which strengtheneth me" (Phil. 4:13).

Do you see yourself as a man who can do all things which God wants him to do? As a man who is bringing himself under control? As a man who will move along for God and get things done for God? As a man who knows the direction he ought to be going, and who knows how to lead people in that direction? As a man who can sustain himself in the midst of difficulties and hardships? If so, it is likely that you have a wholesome, sanctified self-image. And if you find yourself lacking in any of these areas, ask God to help you to be the master of yourself, the master of your work, the master of your responsibilities.

Why not begin to say to yourself: God wants me to be a success in His work. And what God *wants* me to do, I *can* do—and I *will* do! I will be an achiever because God expects it of me. And even now I am, this minute, beginning to do something about it.

Then away with those crutches called excuses! Ours is no place for "the bland leading the bland." Let us bypass the menace of mediocrity in the ministry. Down with "the abominable no-man"! May the go-getter become the go-giver. May the church that had no gains become the marching, winning, growing church because the pastor is willing to stab himself awake and challenge his people to the hilt . . . with a wonderful faith!

Chapter 5

GOOD GROOMING FOR GOD'S MAN

Not only must the minister have a good self-image, he must have an equally strong public image. The self-image deals with the man we do not see, while the public image deals with the man who is visible to all. Perhaps the proportion may be roughly the same as that of an iceberg, yet both are important beyond measure. Laurence Peter has a "Peter's Placebo" which he defines in a sort of tongue-in-cheek way as follows: "An ounce of image is worth a pound of performance."[1]

As Mr. Peter implies, we all see two things: (1) Image is important, and (2) image alone is not enough. Let us see how important it is. A man must not only have the proper concept of himself and his work, he must present himself to the public in a proper manner. Vernon Howard has observed that "the best way to keep cake from getting stale is to wrap it in wax paper and place it near children. The best way to keep yourself in demand is to wrap yourself in your very best personality and place yourself near men."[2]

In considering how a man may wrap himself in his best personality, let us list

10 Facets of the Public Image of the Minister

1. Physical Grooming
This includes hair, clothes, shoes, fingernails, breath,

posture, and personal habits such as scratching the face, etc. There is absolutely no place for slouchiness in the life of a minister, for holiness demands neatness at all times. If the preacher wants to know how he ought to look in public by way of hair and clothes, he would do well to remain current as well as cultured. It is possible to be in step with one's generation without neglecting a holiness standard. A truly holiness standard is at once both demanding and reasonable. A minister, reflecting the image of God, cannot dress in any manner which stresses sensual appeal to the neglect of a godly appearance. As men of God, a minister's physical grooming should reveal Christian harmony in modern fashion styles and a reasonable decorum as well. Neatness and modesty are always guidelines in the appearance of a minister and his family.

2. Personality Grooming

There is no such thing as a "born preacher" or a "born leader." We are all born babies. And although some of us may have to work harder than others at the business of pastoral leadership, all of us develop by self-discipline and diligent application. Personality is never a finished product—it is a divine gift which always needs curbing, stretching, honing, cultivating, improving.

Let the preacher never be guilty of loud talking, coarseness of speech, gossip, criticism, or the fatal fault of "know-it-all-ism." God's man must be approachable, never domineering, never guilty of making alibis for his failure. The timid man needs to correct his timidity and the aggressive one needs to curb his aggressiveness.

3. Domestic Grooming

The way a man acts at home is a fairly accurate index of his true character. Although his wife must share some of the responsibility for the quality of his home life, yet the man is himself responsible for his own household. It is becoming to a man of God to have proper table manners—

never serving himself first, never reaching across the table in front of others, always allowing his wife and other ladies to be seated before he is seated, to place their orders before he places his order. The wife should be treated as the queen of the parsonage and never as the slave of the parsonage. The husband should set the pace for an orderly house.

I sat on a Board of Orders and Relations whose duty it was to examine ministers who were candidates for ordination. On one occasion this board rejected a minister for ordination because (among other reasons, of course) he left his Christmas tree on the front porch until the end of February. On another occasion I saw a similar board delay ordination of a minister because he lacked neatness in personal habits—and in his home.

4. Deportment Grooming

Good manners in the pulpit and out of it are a must for the minister. He should never put his hands in his pockets as a matter of habit. He should check his posture carefully and frequently. Never, under any circumstances, should he be seen chewing gum. He should pay all financial obligations promptly. The reputations of many people in the community have been damaged by thoughtless ministers leaving unpaid bills when they moved from the area. Also, the conduct or the minister with the opposite sex should at all times be above question. Nor should he ever be careless or lazy or indolent.

5. Social Grooming

Ralph Waldo Emerson said that good manners is the ability to put up pleasantly with bad ones. A preacher can't get by with crudeness and thoughtlessness and carelessness in the matters of everyday living. He must always be on time for every occasion. The person who makes others wait on him is actually showing a basic contempt for them. Horace Mann is quoted as having said that un-

43

faithfulness in keeping an appointment is an act of clear dishonesty. You may as well steal a person's money as to steal his time. If a minister is late for an appointment or is tardy in beginning a service, it is a serious mark against him. It reflects on his ability to discipline himself, his home, and his work.

Let the man of God never appear opinionated, infected with self-pride, or possessed with the fatal malady of negativism. Let him be attentive in every conversation. Some preachers are professional book-stealers, although they would not like to be dubbed as such. If a man borrows a book from another's library, he has a definite obligation to return it in good condition, promptly. In fact, it may be a mark against him to be borrowing it in the first place.

6. Friendship Grooming

A preacher is known by the company he keeps. He must choose his ministerial friends wisely, for he will become what they are. It is good to have older friends to instill ideals and to have younger friends to impart enthusiasm. Beware of making friends with the superficial-type minister. If he stumbles and falls by the wayside, you will be sure to be hurt by his fall simply because you are his intimate friend. Avoid close friendships with those who display looseness of speech and action, negativism, liberalism, denominational disloyalty, and shallow commitment.

Cultivate friendships with the men whom you would most like to imitate. Select friends who are most likely to succeed in winning souls to Christ and advancing the kingdom of God. Avoid the critical, the shallow, the insincere, the disloyal. Why not imitate successful men instead of failures? Why follow the follower when you could follow the leader? You will become like those you admire. Keep away from people who would belittle your highest ambitions. Never allow your personality to sag by being with the wrong people.

7. Community Grooming

Do not be afraid to join the ministerial associations and the civic clubs. Although some in these groups do not share your theology or your standards, yet they need your strength and support to make them better. And you can better represent your community by supporting these groups as far as it is possible to do so. Don't shun a liquor fight or a battle against pornography, for you should be at the front of such crusades. Your spiritual assignment demands that you be aggressive in cleaning up sin where you find it. Get acquainted with the leaders in your community, especially the church editor of your newspaper. While ministers should avoid partisan politics, yet they should always be involved in matters of morality and ethics in the community.

8. Pulpit Grooming

Always sit erect, look pleasant, and have the details of the service well under control. Ministers on the platform should not violate the rules of common courtesy by talking during the service. The minister should always display poise, kindness, and a little humor in his message. His services must always begin on time and end on time, regardless of how much time he has to preach. He should avoid scolding and negativism in his pulpit utterances. Nor should he spend his time exhorting, begging, and pleading. He must, of course, be forever on guard against incorrect grammar.

His announcements, if printed in the pew bulletin, need not be repeated from the pulpit. If there is no printed bulletin, his announcements should be very brief and carefully thought out. It denotes lack of thorough preparation for the minister to call for (or encourage) announcements from the people in the congregation during the morning or evening services. The people should be informed that all announcements are to be handed to the pastor in writing before the service starts. Let the minister's wife never be guilty of correcting her husband regarding announcements (or any other matters) during the services.

Orderliness in the service does not mean that allowance cannot be made for outpourings of spiritual blessing such as spontaneous testimonies. But these should be the exception, else they lose their meaning and effectiveness. One more thing, let the pastor always place his tithe envelope in the collection plate each Sunday—just as he encourages the members to do, for his example at this point is always important.

9. Leadership Grooming

Since the pastor is the leader of the church, the chairman of the church board, and president of the church meetings, it is imperative that his executive etiquette show through well. The business meetings should not only begin and end on time, but be conducted in correct form. A well-prepared agenda should be distributed at the opening of the meetings. As chairman of these meetings, the pastor should not allow talkative members of the group to divert attention from the main business of the meeting. Much of the work could be done ahead of time in committees and be referred to the entire group in the form of recommendations. Goals should be set at the grass roots level rather than be dictated from the top. Responsibility and authority should be delegated by the pastor to the proper people. New blood should be added regularly. And above all, let the pastor remember that the best informed people make the best choices.

10. Denominational Grooming

Success is a cooperative venture in the Church of Jesus Christ. The minister is a part of a larger group of ministers, pastors, evangelists, teachers, missionaries, and others who are laboring together to accomplish God's will in the world. Therefore there is no place in the ministry for "lone-wolfism," or for the man who proposes to take care of only his local responsibilities. The wider interests of district, zone, denomination, and community outreach should all receive their due attention. All of these together are a part of the work of the pastor. In this cooperative effort he has serious responsibilities. Thus, the pastor should attend all zone meetings, district meetings, and area meetings of his denomination.

The effective pastor pays all his budgets and apportionments in full, on time, regularly. All reports are treated as important and are filled out and mailed before deadlines. If the pastor challenges his people to pay their various budgets and obligations, the people almost always accept that challenge.

There is no place for ministerial jealousy in God's work; no place for exaggeration of attendance figures or financial reports. The minister must avoid the trap of letting mail go unanswered. He should open *all* his mail in the first place.

When a minister leaves a church, he ought to leave it, period. He should not try to control it and operate it or to conduct its funerals and weddings after he has resigned as pastor. Nor should the minister serve too many years on one district. He should be willing and wise enough to branch out into pastorates in other sections of the country. Ministers who stay a long time in one small area will sooner or later be limited in their ability to relocate. Wider contacts in other areas will assure him of a broader field of service and at the same time keep him free from ruts. The minister always places responsibility before security, paying attention to Gen. Douglas MacArthur's injunction: "Servicemen have no security, only responsibility."

Such are some of the facets of good grooming of God's

man. Perhaps the words of Strickland Gillian will give us a fitting final word at this point:

> Just stand aside and watch yourself go by;
> Think of yourself as "he" instead of "I."
> Note, closely, as another man you note,
> The bag-kneed trousers and the seedy coat;
> Pick flaws; find fault; forget the man is you,
> And strive to make your estimate ring true;
> Confront yourself and look you in the eye—
> Just stand aside and watch yourself go by.[3]

Chapter 6

THE MENACE OF MEDIOCRITY

I shall not soon forget our first trip up Pikes Peak—the gravel road, the ancient car, the steep inclines, the thick pall of dust, but above all, at the top, the vast panorama of enchantment stretching many miles in every direction. At the halfway house one trembling member of our party got out of the car and refused to get back in. "I'll wait right here till you get back—*if* you ever get back!" she said crisply. It was too much for this flat-lander! So she waited in safety while the others of us took the high road with all its fearful risks—and never-to-be-forgotten, breathtaking beauty.

The word *mediocre* literally means "halfway up a mountain." It tells of the ordinary. It describes the halfway-house sort of fellow who is content with a small achievement and afraid of greater—failing to attempt the high road to more worthy accomplishments. Mediocrity is a menace—more for the minister than for any other person because of the spiritual nature of his calling. Let us examine two or three areas in which mediocrity is a menace to the minister.

A. 10 Blind Spots in Pastoral Leadership

1. Opposition. Some pastors do not know how to handle it. They have not learned to cope with the no vote. As a consequence, their frustrations lead them to wrong choices and irrational conclusions. Sometimes they will quit and run to greener pastures. Sometimes they will fight back, trying to subdue opposition. Sometimes they will try to get those who oppose them out of the church. God's way is to kill them—kill them with love.

2. Leadership turnover. New blood is an imperative. Change is a must. Some churches have not had a new member elected to the church board in 10 years—while others are being upset too often. Moderation is the rule. In larger churches a rotation system may help.

3. Communication. Some pastors excel here while some fail miserably. A pastor must be able to talk openly with his people and they with him. I know a case where people have come from board meetings in tears or where they have simply walked out to join other churches or denominations. It is not enough for pastors to be good men —they must be good communicators—and communication is a two-way street.

4. Ignoring the clock. Evangelists sometimes preach too long—as do some pastors. It is a mistake for a preacher to think his sermon is all-important. It is results which are all-important. And long-winded sermons nullify results very rapidly.

5. Delegating. Some pastors have forgotten how to farm out their work. They would rather run the mimeograph than teach someone else how to do it. The crying need of the church in this hour is to harness the saints in whatever capacity for God's harvest.

6. Goals. As surely as insurance companies need goals, the church needs them. As surely as automobile manufacturers promote new cars, so should the church promote the old-time gospel. As surely as doctors and nurses need training to heal the sick, so do preachers and laymen need training to win the lost to Christ.

7. *"Everybody understands our doctrine."* This is among the darkest of all blind spots. If your church is getting any new people at all, these new people do not understand our doctrine unless we preach it often to them. Our own children do not understand unless we teach them. Let's preach holiness clearly and often!

8. *Small-church complex.* Some preachers—and laymen—have a growth block. They fail to see that it is either growth or stagnation—life or death. The church that has no net gain in 12 months should change its methods or change its leaders—or both!

9. *Roll-cleaning.* Recently a pastor showed me a list of more than 180 names which was given him the first week in his new pastorate. The person who gave him the list said, "The former pastor wants you to remove all these names from the church membership roll, for many are dead, are in Florida or California, or simply cannot be found. Most have not attended for years." Up until that moment this church had been the largest on the district. Rolls should be honest, but roll-cleaning should be approached with caution, remembering the redemptive mission of the church.

10. *Integrity.* This must be at the top of the list for all who name the name of Christ. Holy living demands it. Let the figures be always accurate. Let there be no "smoke" regarding the morals of the man of God. Let no smut come upon his lips. May he never be accused of manipulating a brother pastor out of his pastorate so that he may get that pastorate for himself. May he never "forget" to pay a bill or a debt. May he never shade the truth or twist the facts. Power, money, and illicit sex are the three areas

where men of the world most often fall. May the man of God be on guard at all times. Integrity is the key.

It has been said that ministers die from the inside out and from the top down. I submit that they come alive the same way.

In our further consideration of the menace of mediocrity in the lives of ministers, let us turn our attention to

B. 11 False Philosophies

1. False security. "I'll make a bundle on the side," said one preacher whose church was paying him a not-too-good salary. And of course there are times when pastors —or their wives—find it necessary to supplement their salaries with secular employment. But financial security is always a false security for ministers.

2. False leadership. "If they do not respond, I'll not put up with them," said one pastor glibly; "I'll run them off." Said another: "Anyone who loved the former pastor has no place of leadership in my administration." Both were dead wrong. Both have a decaying usefulness.

3. Hollow call. "My call to preach is flexible. I can serve God any place I choose—whether in the active ministry or not. I can still fulfill my call even if I become a layman." Such fallacious thinking is fatal to any minister.

4. False freedom. "If I disagree with the standards or the doctrines of my church, I have a right to put on a campaign to get these changed." Hardly! Can you imagine an astronaut saying, "If I do not like the course chosen for me to go to the moon, I am free to change it to suit my own pleasure"?

5. False humility. One pastor was told, "Don't use your talents at writing or speaking if you think you are going to be advanced thereby." Jesus made the opposite emphasis when He congratulated the five-talent man for developing his talents to the full.

6. *Pseudohonesty*. "Let's be honest and slash these membership rolls to the bone and put spirituality above numbers," said one thoughtless young pastor full of idealism. But it is a false honesty if it causes some to be forever lost who may have been embittered on hearing they were removed from the church fellowship. Even holiness churches do not claim that all their members are as holy as they ought to be. But we do not help them by cutting them off.

7. *False harmony*. "Don't stick your neck out— peace and harmony are all-important in God's work. Let's avoid trouble. No use getting voted out—even if the issue is fundamental." Does that sound like the way the Apostle Paul operated?

8. *False pride*. "Forget appearance. Don't spend so much time and money on a fine house and nice clothes. It's spirituality that counts." Wrong again! God expects us to *look* like children of the King! Spiritual people ought to have the neatest, best-dressed home in the block! And that doesn't mean it has to be the most expensive.

9. *False motivation*. "Why work so hard? They will not appreciate you any more for it." Remember: our motivation goes beyond the appreciation of the people, for we are seeking the approval of God. A complete consecration involves hard work!

10. *Optional responsibility*. "My budgets are too big, so I think I'll just let the big churches pay them. Besides, our local church has not voted to assume these budgets." We believe in budgets because we believe in the Great Commission. Why not say: "Let's pay our fair share—and more if we can do it"?

11. *False methods*. "Let's forget all this promotional stuff and just get out and win souls." Would a coal miner

forget all his tools and just dig coal without them? Effective pastors seek out every possible tool and method to facilitate their task.

Henry Wadsworth Longfellow said it this way:

Not in the clamor of the crowded street,
Not in the shouts and plaudits of the throng
But in ourselves, are triumph and defeat.

Now let us examine the menace of ministerial mediocrity by considering the aspect of failure.

C. Failure Is a By-product

Like success, failure is a by-product of some prior concept or action or philosophy. Both usually come gradually and according to definable steps and laws. Both success and failure are consequences. Both have causes. Both are by-products of some former action taken. And unlike success, failure is unintended and unexpected.

F. W. Boreham is quoted as having said, "Some men are called to preach; some are not called to preach; and some are called not to preach." Our consideration here is limited to those in the first category: those who are called to preach. God does not intend nor does He will their failure. Why, then, do some fail? I am indebted to Dr. V. H. Lewis for some of the ideas here mixed with my own.

1. Unsustained self-motivation. Failure is the by-product of a man's inability to sustain self-motivation in the face of inertia, failures, pressures, and unappreciative peers.

2. Mind-set of negativism. Failure is the by-product of a ministerial mind-set of negativism and fatalism and gloom that possesses some people in God's work. You have seen them walk, heads down and shoulders bent. You have heard them say, "Nothing can be done in this wicked community."

3. *Tyranny of laziness.* Failure is the by-product of that terrifying tyranny of laziness that fetters some people. Those who would be effective in God's work are like the young executive who said: "I want to do more than the boss requires. Satisfactory performance is simply not enough to suit me. I can't take the attitude that 'it's just a job, and I'll do what I can.' My basic drive is for excellence —the standard I want to meet." [1]

4. *Results without causes.* Failure is the by-product of expecting promotions and results without sufficient causes. I heard Earl Nightingale say in a speech that "if you are not worth more than you are *now* receiving, you cannot move ahead . . . you are already receiving all you are worth."

5. *Seduced by the secular.* Failure is the by-product of the call to conform to the world—of being seduced by the secular. A friend and I were discussing the moral failure of an acquaintance when my friend said to me: "He is a victim of the times—rampant rottenness on every hand." But I believe we both knew that the failure could have been avoided—in spite of the times. His peers had not succumbed.

6. *Juggling of priorities.* Failure is the by-product of the juggling of priorities—of placing first things second-- of misplacing values. The price tags have been swapped. Review is imperative or the crash is inevitable. When my sainted mother was 92 years old, she wrote this to me on the occasion of my birthday:

> I thank God every day for you and for what you are trying to do in His kingdom . . . for the opportunities given you from time to time to proclaim His Word, and to be a help to your men on the job. In all these things walk side-by-side with Him who knew no sin. Beware of the many church honors bestowed on you, lest you become vain. After all, we are just mud, or dust, owing to the weather.

7. *Camouflaging of inadequacies.* Failure is the by-product of the camouflaging of inadequacies with alibis and bluster. It reminds us of the note on the edge of the preacher's sermon outline reading: "Yell loudly here—argument is weak."

8. *Self-sympathy.* Failure is the by-product of resting too much in the shade of the juniper tree of self-sympathy. How easily some indulge this when opposition mounts and votes go against them. And how fatal!

9. *Personal prestige above God's work.* Failure is the by-product of destroying God's work to salvage our own prestige. This is done by eliminating opposition immediately before the crucial vote—of stepping on people to get ahead.

10. *Status quoism.* Failure is the by-product of the deadly malady of status quoism—the idea that if we are holding our own we are getting ahead—that growth is not important anyway. Henry Ford turned it around when he said that the man who will see how much he can give for a dollar instead of how little he can give for a dollar, will succeed.

11. *Benefits without responsibilities.* Failure is the by-product of the willingness to accept the benefits of our ministry without assuming the responsibilities of our ministry. A prospective preacher once wrote to C. B. Jernigan, saying he was "looking for a place where he could succeed." The answer from Jernigan was simple: "The preachers who succeed in Oklahoma are men who take the bull by the horns, break his neck, skin him, make a tent of his hide, peddle the meat for a living while they preach holiness. Come on over and I will show you the pasture where the bull runs."[2]

12. *Inadequate resources.* Failure is the by-product of having inadequate resources to achieve Kingdom objectives. Courage is required to stand against evil and for

righteousness. God's man must be able to challenge lay inertia and effectively persuade men for God.

13. *Ebb tide of lost romance.* Failure is the by-product of sinking with the ebb tide of a lost romance. The preaching becomes a hollow shell. Holiness becomes a dead correctness. The call is questioned. The preacher is open to compromise and temptation. Jim Elliot, martyr of Ecuador, had this to say: "Am I ignitible? God deliver me from the dead asbestos of 'other things.' Saturate me with the oil of the Spirit that I may be a flame. Make me Thy fuel, Flame of God!"[3]

Admittedly this has been a rather negative appraisal of the menace of mediocrity, of the blind spots in pastoral leadership, of some false philosophies and areas of failure. But we need to get down to bedrock, to begin to eradicate from our lives the things that keep us from advancement in Christ's worthy work. And may God bring us to noble achievements!

Chapter 7

A SENSE OF STRATEGY

"Get all your ducks in a row," was a favorite saying of a fine board member in a church I once pastored in Kansas City. He enjoyed telling the story of the old hunter who had only one piece of lead shot left. He poured the exact amount of powder into the old muzzle-loader, then waited until he sighted five ducks all in a row. The bullet went right through the head of each duck, finally lodging in the fifth head. "Get all your ducks in a row," he repeated, "and you can bag all five with one shot with no waste of powder and even retrieve your bullet for another shot. And you don't tear up the meat, either!" Although M. Frank Turner was not much of a duck hunter, he applied this sense of strategy to his business and became a success. And by his example we applied it to church affairs—with gratifying results.

If the minister is to be an effective leader of men, he must make a lifelong study of people and methods. Thus he will develop a sense of strategy which will help him find his way along in church administration and human relationships.

In the following paragraphs will be found some precepts which were gleaned from the writings of Joseph D.

Cooper in his excellent book, *The Art of Decision Making.*[1] I have added some of my own.

1. *Accumulate Pertinent Information*

The pastor will wish to gather key information, not only each time he enters a new pastorate, but constantly and systematically throughout each pastorate. The minister will have access to records and should dig in until he locates all the necessary information of the past and the present. He needs to know his people: where they work, how they live, their strengths and weaknesses. He should know each department of the church—studying areas of progress and failure and projecting possibilities for the future. He ought to know each individual Sunday school teacher and class officer and also the records of each class. He should know people well enough to place the right ones in the right places of leadership responsibility.

Information about the growth of his church through the years and its record of achievements is also important to the pastor. He may wish to know something of the financial strength of the church—and of its potential in this area. He ought to avail himself of the record of contributions of each individual, though some may feel that having such knowledge might color his attitudes and also his preaching. Based on these records, the pastor should prepare (or have prepared) charts and graphs to chart progress and future goals. The pastor should be the best-informed man in the church concerning its inner workings.

2. *Fill In the Blank Spaces Accurately*

It is quite possible that some of the records or facts will not be available. There will be gaps and blank spaces. The pastor will need to be able to round out and properly fill in the information. He will learn to look at the overall pattern and from that make his own deductions. This will be true not only about facts and figures but also about personalities and people. At this point he will need to exercise great caution lest he make erroneous judgments. I recall the story of the lad who came to his father with his report card and said, "Dad, I don't want to scare you, but the teacher said if I didn't get better grades somebody is sure to get spanked." Wrong conclusions can bring additional problems.

3. *Frame the Issues Clearly*

The minister must learn how to interpret the facts as well as to see them. Perception is all-important here. He must learn how to relate facts to one another. He should be able to see the events of the past in sequence and bring himself up-to-date in regard to the program and the present progress of the church. He should be able to focus on the issues clearly in relation to problems in the church. He will certainly not jump to unwarranted conclusions.

4. *See the Whole Picture*

I remember as a lad the first time I climbed high in a live oak tree. What fun it was to look down on cows and horses. Then I climbed the windmill and looked down on our big two-story house. Then there came the first trip to the city skyscraper—my first airplane ride—and at last the seven-mile-high jet flight. The view from the heights enabled me to see things in a way I had never seen them before. Perspective is a must in church leadership, too. If he is to make correct judgments, the minister must be able to see the whole picture. He can do this only if he saturates his mind with pertinent data. Some of us are like the poet's description of the lightning bug:

> *The lightning bug is brilliant,*
> *But he hasn't any mind;*
> *He blunders through existence*
> *With his headlight on behind.*[2]

By seeing the whole picture the pastor can learn to fit the pieces of his problem together in jigsaw fashion. Good perspective will keep him from snap judgments of problems or people.

5. *Locate the Central Issues*

The effective pastor, if he is to have an adequate sense of strategy, must be able to weed out items of lesser concern and get to the heart of the issue. He will not let himself be distracted by the side issues. I recall the story of a man who stopped fighting the fire that was consuming his house in order that he might kill a rat that was running down the street. The rat should have been destroyed, of course, but that was hardly the central issue confronting the man at the moment. His house was on fire! Aldous Huxley pointed out that facts do not cease to exist because they are ignored.

6. *Inform the People*

The adequate pastor sees the vital importance of clear communication. He knows that informed people make the best choices, so he seeks to get the message through. Many worthy programs have failed because of a breakdown between pastor and people. Is it a tithing campaign? A building program? A reorganization idea that needs to be "sold" to the people? Then the people must know all the details. This can best be done through patient distribution of literature, the assembling of facts and figures, and, of course, pulpit pronouncements.

I once knew of a young pastor who was confronted by a serious financial deficit. At a meeting of the church board he told them, "Keep it quiet—don't let anyone know, for this is embarrassing." So they kept it quiet and matters worsened . . . until at last the young pastor was forced to make known the need from the pulpit. The people responded and cleared up the deficit—as they would have earlier had he levelled with them. Spiritual people will respond when they know all the facts.

7. *Organize Logically*

Organization is not an enemy to spirituality: it is a friend. Jesus showed this when He sent out the 70 workers, all organized and instructed for the purpose of witnessing and winning souls (Luke 10). People will more likely get involved if they are organized in their assignments. Of course organization often calls for groundwork—committees, job descriptions, delegation of authority and responsibility, and follow-up. If duties are spelled out reasonably and logically, and if assignments are given with precision, it is likely that less friction will occur and more work will be accomplished. I have before me financial policies and job descriptions and programs which successful pastors have formulated—through appropriate boards and committees—to advance the local church. Where these are lacking, leadership is lacking—and trouble is almost inevitable.

8. *Control the Elements of Decision Making*

I observed a church which was stymied for years by one man's negative influence. There was no growth, no progress, no harmony. Pastors came and left without seeing the picture change. Every major forward move was put on the shelf by the influence of this one person. The people did not want it to be this way, but no one seemed to find a way to change things.

Then came a pastor who introduced a tithing campaign. Although Mr. Big could not afford to oppose tithing, he did not sign up. Then came a proposal for relocation. This he publicly opposed, so the pastor resorted to the secret ballot on every vote. Thus the people who had been afraid to vote yes by show of hands now voted yes by ballot, because they were not afraid of being exposed to the man who had so long dominated their thinking.

Much thought should be given by the minister before he enters into a given project or course of action. He needs to know with fair assurance where he will come out before he starts digging the tunnel. Indeed, he needs to know what kinds of difficulties he will run into as he proceeds. Without being a domineering dictator, a pastor, as any other executive, must have a sense of strategy in this particular area of controlling the elements of decision making.

For instance, if the pastor sees a negative element assuming leadership in the church and has a project in mind which could be opposed, he must move with great caution. Perhaps he should delay the issue rather than hazard the wrong decision. This course puts a tremendous responsibility on the pastor and means he will have to face up to the consequences of his actions. Perhaps decisions can be controlled by two basic steps: (1) informing the people over a period of time, and (2) using the straw ballot before the official ballot is taken.

In one of my pastorates I recognized a need for a building program but was informed that a negative decision had already been made by the congregation and that nothing could be done about it. So I waited. When the time seemed ripe, we began taking straw ballots in the church board meetings. The people were apparently unanimous in their desire to explore the idea of relocation. It was the first small step in the direction we wanted to go. Later other larger steps were taken until finally the job was accomplished in good fashion. Timing is always an important factor in directing the decision-making process.

9. *Keep the Institutional Perspective*

The church must always keep in mind that it is a *church* and not a business enterprise. Let the saints be constantly aware that they are a part of a larger fellowship—a larger group of churches. They are not completely independent. Rudyard Kipling said it in this brief verse:

> *For the strength of the Pack is the Wolf,*
> *And the strength of the Wolf is the Pack.*

63

Let the church ever be aware of the ultimate goals to which the saints are committed and the methods by which these goals should be reached. The effective pastor is always reminding his people that they have two guidelines: the Holy Bible and the church *Manual.* Strong churches are built on these two foundations. God pity the pastor who would lead his people (or allow his people to be led) away from the strong moorings of his denominational standards or doctrines. While no denomination is perfect, we always gain when we attempt to strengthen it rather than turn away from its basic tenets. Our ultimate goals are clearly outlined in God's Word.

10. *Maintain Objectivity*

It is important that the pastor occasionally stand back and look critically at his performance. Cultivating objectivity is basic to a sense of strategy. It is good if the pastor can become critical of his own procedures and methods and results—even skeptical. Someone has observed that if a man has done a certain thing for a certain way for five years, he ought to carefully and critically review it. After some years he ought to throw it away and start all over again. John Wesley is quoted as saying that after a preacher has preached the same sermons for 10 years he ought to burn them and dig out new ones. All of which means that preachers can keep themselves and their churches out of ruts if they will be honestly objective.

Chapter 8

TECHNIQUES OF ANTICIPATION

Perhaps you have noticed that on the sides of the face of a cat are long whiskers sticking out in both directions. As a lad I was at times tempted to take the scissors and cut them off to see what would happen. In later years, however, I was told that these cat's whiskers are for his guidance in going through narrow places. If the animal starts through an opening and discovers that his whiskers do not clear it, then he backs up, knowing that he cannot get his whole body through. These whiskers are feelers to protect him from possible trouble. One preacher described another by saying: "He has cat's whiskers a mile long." What he meant was: "That man can sense trouble a long way off— and he knows how to get around it."

Let us consider here some techniques of anticipation —cat's whiskers, if you please—which will help us as we move along in our work.

1. *Fix Dates*

The more than 100 churches on the Northeastern Indiana District have agreed upon a three-year district calendar. The dates are established well in advance and all other functions must be worked around these. The calendar is set up in a chronological listing and also by interest groups so that anyone can look ahead for any number of years and determine dates of district events. It is published each year for three years in advance.

Many local churches also project dates ahead so that members may plan their vacations and other personal plans without fear of conflict with the local church activities. People appreciate knowing what is going to happen next month and next year and two or three years in advance. These dates should be set by the church board members and departmental leaders and other responsible people, in harmony with the suggestions of the pastor, of course. Thus regular church board meetings, revivals, committee meetings, planning groups, zone and district gatherings, conventions, and any other activities involving church members are dated well in advance. The calendar should be published and/or posted so people may plan accordingly.

2. *Study Trends*

The alert pastor is ever seeking out problems before they grow large, and converting them into challenges. This is best done by a constant study of trends in the local church. By glancing at his own charts and graphs, the minister readily observes trends and tendencies in areas of finance, attendance, enrollment, membership, new converts, and other items relating to church growth. He needs to watch these reports carefully and be sensitive to everything that is happening in the church.

Of course there are some areas which cannot be charted, such as spiritual victories, worldly tendencies, and such intangibles. But by carefully observing these tides, the pastor can more intelligently pray, preach, and plan. Church board members and perhaps other officers should be alerted to trends in the church so that they can join the pastor in his concerns—and help him to find solutions.

3. *Have an Ear for Rumblings*

The effective pastor will always keep his ear to the ground for discontent, rumblings, and dissension. This is not to say that the pastor ought to have a spy system in the church—snooping out all who are opposed to his program. But he ought to be alert enough to know what is being said and what is happening in the hearts of his people. He needs to know how his programs are being accepted.

He needs to know the attitudes of his people on matters of current interest outside the church as well as developments within the congregation. No pastor can afford to blind himself to the thinkings, feelings, and opinions of his people. If he keeps himself informed of potential problems, he can often handle them before they get out of hand. He can best do this by developing a sort of sixth sense—an ability to understand what people are thinking and to feel their support or opposition. To do this, he must live close to God and close to his people—and carefully listen.

4. *Build a Checklist*

The pastor has so many hats to wear that he needs a place to hang them—a checklist to see that each responsibility is cared for, each deadline is met, each gap is bridged. The schedule of fixed dates is a good beginning place, but it needs to be broken down into more detail—into weekly chunks and daily bites and maybe hourly bits. In this way he can anticipate what is about to happen (except emergencies), be more effective, and use his time more wisely. Dr. James B. Chapman once said, "Push your work or your work will push you."

5. *Enlist Strong Leaders*

I once had occasion to observe a pastor who was not a strong leader and therefore was afraid to use the ablest men in his congregation. They were a threat to him. The first year in a certain pastorate he eased out all the able men who were in office and filled his major places of leadership with men of lesser caliber. Needless to say, morale sagged and unrest developed. Many fine people left that church and joined others. Wise leaders will gather around them men stronger than themselves. In almost every congregation there are people who could be developed into strong leaders. The best way to discover a man's potential is to put him to work. And most spiritual people are willing to work if challenged to do so.

A businessman once observed that the best manager is the one who has wisdom enough to pick good men to do what he wants done, and self-restraint enough to keep from meddling with them as they do it.

6. *Delegate Responsibility*

Harold T. Jackson of Canton, Ohio, vice-president of Nationwide Insurance Company, says, "We are leading successfully when we are getting people to do the work we want them to do, in the way we want it done, when we want it done, because they want to do it." There is doubtless an unemployment balance in your church. The pastor and a few dedicated saints are doing much of the work while many other good people are doing little or nothing for their church. The way to get more work done is to put more people to work. The way to put more people to work is to train them, assign them, give them job descriptions, give them authority and responsibility, with occasional reporting back.

In their excellent book, *The Techniques of Delegating,* Donald A. and Eleanor C. Laird give us the following tongue-in-cheek picture of delegating:

Executives are a fortunate lot. For, as everybody knows, an executive has nothing to do. That is, except . . .

To decide what is to be done;
To tell somebody to do it;
To listen to reasons why it should not be done, why it

68

should be done by somebody else, or why it should be done a different way;

And to prepare arguments and rebuttal that are convincing and conclusive;

To follow up to see if the thing has been done;

To discover that it has not been done;

To inquire why it has not been done;

To listen to excuses from the person who should have done it and did not do it;

And to think up arguments to overcome excuses . . .

To follow up the second time to see if the thing has been done;

To discover that it was done, but done incorrectly;

To point out how it should have been done;

To conclude that as long as it has been done it might as well be left the way it is;

To wonder if it isn't time to get rid of a person who never does anything correctly;

To reflect that the person at fault has a wife and seven children;

And that certainly no other executive in the world would put up with him for a moment;

And that in all probability any successor would be just as bad, or worse;

To consider how much simpler and better the thing would have been done had he done it himself in the first place;

To reflect sadly that if he had done it himself he would have been able to do it right in twenty minutes;

Whereas, as it turned out, it took someone else three weeks to do it incorrectly;

But, to realize that had he done it himself,

It would have had a very demoralizing effect on the whole organization,

Because it would strike at the very fundamental belief of all employees

That an executive has nothing to do![1]

7. *Set Goals*

Someone has said: "Aim high! It won't be any harder on your gun to knock the tail feathers out of an eagle than to splinter a barn door!" Perhaps it should be observed that if a person aims before pulling the trigger, he is more likely to hit the barn door (or the bird) than if he just pulls the trigger aimlessly.

Goal setting is a challenging responsibility for the pastor. He needs to know *why* goals are to be set, the *kinds* of goals that are helpful, the *time element* in goal setting, *who* should be involved in the process, and *how*.

 a. *Why* goals are to be set:
     To narrow the range of our effort
     To bring our work into clear focus
     To make our endeavors more logical
     To measure our progress
 b. *Kinds* of goals that are helpful:
     Financial
     Numerical
     Physical
     Organizational
     Spiritual
 c. *Time element* in goal setting:
     Short-range goals (under one year)
     Intermediate goals (one to five years)
     Long-range goals (over five years)
 d. *Who* should set goals:
     Each person, his personal goals
     Leaders plus members, goals for the group
 e. *How* should goals be set:
     Seldom from the top
     Help subordinates work out goals
     Grass-roots participation

8. *Motivate—Don't Dictate*

It is impossible for a leader to antagonize and motivate at the same time. While the pastor's big responsibility is to get the church moving ahead, his big problem is to find out how this can be accomplished. Sometimes in his

70

impatience the minister is tempted to push the people along—and people do not like to be pushed. However, they will usually follow the leader if he is worthy.

When President Eisenhower held his first cabinet meeting after taking office, he laid a piece of string on his desk and tried to push it with a finger. But the piece of string piled up in a knot. Then he straightened out the piece of string again, and with his finger on one end, pulled it along on the desk. He was illustrating to his cabinet members that it is better to lead people than to push them. Pushing is often disastrous.

The pastor will soon discover that high-pressure methods and bulldozer procedures are entirely unacceptable in church circles. His real challenge is to motivate rather than to dictate. He will be a want-creator—making people want to help him get his job done. This comes not by argument but through emotions.

9. *Avoid Default at Deadline*

As a consequence of delegation, there needs to be a checkup of performance. In harmony with the principles of motivation, the minister will need to see that his subordinates do not build up to a default at deadline. This will mean that he must keep a close check on all who work with him and carry responsibility, offering assistance where it is needed, and spotting failure where it is occurring. He will seek to help people in these areas rather than allow them the embarrassment of failure at accounting time.

Sometimes a mere mechanical change in procedures will be helpful. It is far better to help people before they get into trouble rather than to try to help them out of it. At this point reaching goals becomes secondary and saving people becomes primary. When the minister saves a man from failure, he saves him from having a cheap idea of himself. He might also be saving him from the bitterness of frustration and from ultimately becoming a dropout in the kingdom of God.

10. *Give Recognition and Awards*

Much is said about gratitude in God's Word, for this is one of the most important factors in the Christian life—and in any life for that matter. Even a dog will love a person who shows him appreciation. Certainly this is the key to the heart of a child. But we need to remember that adults—even spiritual and mature people—appreciate earned gratitude. When a person does a good job, he deserves commendation. Sometimes recognition should be given even if he does not achieve greatly. There will be more achievement-hungry people around if some form of gratitude is expressed when people achieve. If performance is (as someone has said) ability times motivation, then let us remember that recognition for a job well done is actually the best kind of motivation. Nor do the awards need to be fabulous. Public recognition, a firm handclasp, an expression of appreciation, or even some token material gift—these are effective ways of rewarding a person for endless hours of hard work.

Frequently when appreciation is shown by the pastor, other members of the congregation are challenged to greater achievements than ever before. All of which reminds us that we should not only love our enemies, we should treat our friends a little better.

Chapter 9

THE MINISTER AS EXECUTIVE

A Sicilian-born immigrant to the United States, Joe is an example of the type of thing that can happen to someone, because something happened *in* him.

Trouble in the streets, trouble in school, trouble at home. It was a pattern. He left home at 14, lost nearly 40 jobs, and was bankrupt at 35. *Success* magazine, in relating his story, stated that, like many other ghetto-trapped youths in Detroit, he had neither hope nor money.

What happened *to* Joe Girard isn't important for our interests. What happened *in* him is. In 1964, he was the number-one car salesman in Detroit. In 1965, he was the number-one car salesman in his three-state region. In 1967, he sold more cars than anyone in the world, once selling a high of 18 new cars in a single day. In 1973 he sold 1,425 automobiles. He stated his philosophy of life in these words: "I'm motivated solely by want." Motivation is what happens *in* a person—and that makes all the difference in outward performance.

So it must be for the minister. To the degree that a pastor is motivated to accomplish his goals, to that degree will he be a good leader. In an age when leaders can get by with no less than quality leadership-credibility, pastors are forced to constantly reevaluate their strengths and weaknesses in public relations, in individual character assessment, and in any field related to human behavior. If the business and professional worlds make concentrated efforts to establish healthy patterns of following and leading, what about the body of Christ? Pastors have an obligation to review their ability to serve as shepherds. Furthermore, the shepherd-duty of a pastor is not in conflict with his task as preacher, teacher, soul winner, etc. Let us consider some vital areas related to executive skill.

A. Executive Skill in Developing Church Membership

It is the pastor's duty and privilege to build the body of Christ. Here are some guidelines relative to the preparation of converts for church membership:

1. Be sure that new converts are genuinely converted.

2. Enroll them in a pastor's class on church membership. Carefully study the *Manual* in this class, thoroughly review the church's doctrinal statements, be able to support with scripture what the church believes, and be willing to entertain their questions. Nothing related to a healthy, Spirit-filled life-style should be omitted.

3. Inform them of the duties and responsibilities *any* Christian should embrace in general, and the necessity of building upon the church's collective conscience as well as individual convictions.

4. Do not keep them waiting too long to join. Some may be ready to join within days after conversion. Others, depending upon background, may take longer. Children should attend classes on membership taught on their level of comprehension.

5. Joining the church should mean something. All attempts must be made to make the *act* of membership as meaningful as the *action* of being a member ought to be.

6. Make much of Membership Sunday. Read joyously

from the *Manual* and have the new members make their vows at the altar of the church.

7. Involve them in the church program. Make sure they receive the church periodicals. Supply them with a box of tithing envelopes. Emphasize commitment to the task of building the Kingdom through the church. Encourage loyalty, faithfulness, mutual helpfulness.

B. Executive Skill in Holding Church Members

In an eight-quadrennia profile* of the gains and losses in church membership of the Church of the Nazarene, an effort was made to determine both the how and why of the losses, as well as what could be done to hold the gains. Of 150 survey letters mailed, 98 responders marked the following top responses to this question: "Why do we lose them?" in the order given here:

We have failed to get them sanctified wholly soon after conversion.

We need to be more effective in calling them to a committed life.

We have been careless in visiting in their homes soon after they have joined.

We have not harnessed them immediately into church work.

We have not brought them through a pastor's class on membership.

We have been slow in teaching them the standards of the church.

We have failed to give them a sense of belonging to the family of God.

The second part of this survey gave individuals an opportunity to respond to the question "How can we keep them?" A sampling of suggestions are listed:

*This report was prepared by the author just one month prior to his death and was presented posthumously at the Conference of Superintendents, Kansas City, Mo., Jan. 23, 1975.

Keep our motives straight: Win people to save souls rather than meet goals.

Involve them in Bible study immediately after they join, if not before.

Get them involved in meaningful and productive service.

Keep a glowing, spiritual, anointed atmosphere in every service.

Do a better job of preaching and teaching holiness at all levels.

Make use of "care groups" or some type of spiritual sponsor so that concern comes from a one-to-one basis; more "shepherds."

Pay attention to their spiritual growth; be able to predict areas of potential weakness (tithe, devotion to commitments, faithfulness, attendance, etc.).

C. Executive Skill in Maintaining Membership Rolls

Some churches are plagued with "deadwood"; others have been "slashed to the bone." A practical, intelligent way of removing names from membership rolls with neither undue haste nor delay needs to be devised. Here are some possible solutions:

1. The membership record book is the responsibility of the pastor.

2. Remove the names of deceased members immediately.

3. Compose two lists of church members: active and inactive, including addresses.

4. Bring the membership roll up to date regarding name changes by marriage, etc.

5. Write letters to all "inactive" members; ascertain their interest in the church.

6. Transfer names of all who have actually joined other churches.

7. Visit personally all local inactive members. Be slow to drop them if they show any interest whatever.

8. Do not be in a hurry to drop names of people you cannot easily locate.

9. Be very slow to remove names of backsliders.

10. Gradually update the membership roll, showing a net gain, however slight, each year.

11. Magnify the fact of new people joining, not the ones being removed.

12. Leave an accurate, detailed account for your successor. Make him glad he followed you.

D. Executive Skill in Handling Board Meetings

1. *How to conduct a board meeting:*

   a. Follow *Manual* procedure in dates, time, organization, etc.

   b. Prepare mimeographed agendas for meetings, following parliamentary rules.

   c. Distribute copies of the treasurer's report to all members.

   d. Limit all meetings to a reasonable length.

   e. Keep business relaxed and positive, yet productive.

   f. Mail copies of minutes to each member within a week.

   g. Furnish each member with a personal notebook for reports, agendas, minutes, etc.

   h. Open and close meetings with devotional period.

2. *How to wreck a board meeting:*

   a. Call the meeting without advance notice.

   b. Keep the purpose of the meeting a secret.

   c. Have no prepared reports, minutes, or agenda.

   d. Squelch all new ideas not on the agenda; inhibit discussion.

   e. Allow the telephone or other outside disturbances to distract you.

f. Ask leading questions and furnish your own answers.

g. Change decisions reached by the board, without consultation.

h. Allow a few people to dominate discussions, or otherwise fail to control discussion.

E. Executive Skill in Handling People

The skillful leader knows that people, especially the "difficult" ones, will not tolerate pushing, driving, and manipulation. If in their pastor they sense a fair and just man in whom they have confidence, leadership will become a partnership. Here are some basic guidelines for the pastor as he seeks to establish himself as a leader of people:

1. Work from a position of strength, from a solid base.

2. Gain all the facts possible about any situation; avoid blindfolded decisions.

3. Never be caught off base; stay close to the Bible, the *Manual,* and parliamentary rules.

4. Calculate and weigh every possible risk.

5. Be aware of loopholes in logic, both your own and those of opposing viewpoint.

6. Have alternative plans if present ones go sour.

7. Be sure of your facts, then be willing to make a "lonely" decision under God's leadership.

8. Strike when the iron is hot; seize the offensive wisely.

9. Never look back, but move ahead. Don't second-guess yourself.

F. Executive Skill and Handling Negativism

Again, the pastor must demonstrate his skill in dealing with any force of negativism which he may encounter.

As one member told me some years ago, "Preacher, I won't be able to come to the board meeting tonight. But you know me; tell them whatever they are for, I am against." He was being facetious, but unfortunately some are really like that. In fact, opposition may arise in any board. What do you do about the no vote?

1. Recognize that a "yes-men" board is probably a weak one anyway.

2. The privilege of voting no is at the heart of democracy. (But just so is the obligation to fall in line with the majority after the vote is taken.)

3. Try to determine whether the opposition is based on principle or upon emotion or personalities involved. Get the proper perspective.

4. Keep kind in attitude, whatever happens. Don't become "unglued."

5. Don't unchristianize the opponent or retaliate in any way.

6. Consider the majority vote to be God's will for this time and situation.

7. Be objective about the situation. Allow time to work, for it is a great healer.

8. Remember that differences of opinion can be held without breaching friendship or communication.

G. Executive Skill in Recruiting Lay Leaders

Having the ability to get the right people in the right place is highly important in any business. In the church it is equally so, but motivation becomes more acute since the workers are on a volunteer basis. The pastor must be able to recognize leadership skills and develop them. He must also be able to recognize leadership breakdowns.

1. *Questions to ask about potential lay leaders:*

a. Does he assume responsibility and follow through well, or does he alibi and pass the buck?

b. Is he flexible or is he brittle and adamant?

c. Is he cooperative and congenial or is he aloof and needs to be "handled with kid gloves"?

d. Does he buckle under adversity and problems or does he hold steady and stick with the job?

e. Is he a team man, working well with others, or is he a loner or dictator?

f. Is he a person of vision, innovative, or is he apathetic and inclined to accept the status quo?

g. Is he a disciplined person with good self-control, or is he careless, unpredictable, moody, or temperamental?

h. Is he optimistic, inspirational, and up-beat in attitude—a morale builder—or is he negative and pessimistic, viewing life from the gloomy side?

i. Is he genuinely spiritual or is he superficial and careless?

2. *When does a leader need to be replaced* (assuming everything possible has been done to get him on the right track)?

a. When he fails to do the job or shows incompetence

b. When he becomes halfhearted about his task or apparently loses interest

c. When he assumes a possessive attitude toward his office

d. If he is not a team man, fails to attend committee meetings, and disregards authority

e. When those under him are unhappy and frustrated

f. When he loses his spiritual experience

H. Executive Skill when You Get to the End of Your Rope

When it seems you cannot do anything else, your skill as a leader can still be in evidence. Such a situation is not a matter of failure but of biding your time, "sparring for openings" as it were. Here are some tested and proven rules to follow under such circumstances:

1. Be patient. Time is on the side of what is right.

2. Maintain a positive spirit, giving common sense an opportunity to surface.

3. Lift up Christ, the Symbol of hope.

4. Be slow to vindicate yourself.

5. Do not jump to conclusions. Someone wrote: "There once was a dog named August, who was always jumping at conclusions. One day he jumped at the conclusion of a mule, and that was the last day of August."

6. Be slow to exercise your authority. The less you use it, the stronger it is.

7. Remain alert to trends. Take a straw ballot often during important stages of any major issue.

8. Be considerate of the views of others.

9. Know when to retreat and when to fight. Some things are not worth fighting for, dying for, or splitting churches over. Some things are!

10. Delay the final showdown until all the surprises are in.

11. Stay on your knees. If most church problems are basically spiritual, most solutions are basically spiritual.

12. Keep your faith-cable connected.

The following poem by Grace Noll Crowell, entitled "Wait," sums up the inner strength any executive of the ministry must desire.

If but one message I may leave behind,
A single word of courage for my kind

It would be this, Oh brother, friend:
Whatever life may bring—what God may send—
No matter whether clouds may lift soon or late;
Take heart and wait!

Despair may tangle darkly at your feet,
Your faith be dimmed, and hope, once cool and sweet
Be lost. But suddenly, above a hill,
A heavenly lamp set on a heavenly sill
Will shine for you and point the way to go.
How well I know!

For I have waited through the dark, and I
Have seen a star rise in the blackest sky,
Repeatedly; it has not failed me yet.
And I have learned God will not forget
To light His lamp. If we but wait for it
It will be lit! *

*In *Poems of Inspiration and Courage,* by Grace Noll Crowell. Copyright 1936 by Harper and Row, Publishers, Inc. Renewed 1964 by Grace Noll Crowell. By permission of the publishers.

PART TWO

THE FINE ART OF
DEVELOPING LAY LEADERSHIP

Provide . . . able men . . . and place
such over them, to be rulers.
—Exod. 18:21

Chapter 10

MEN OF DISTINCTION

The full-page ad placed by a certain liquor company in a national magazine pictured an elegantly dressed, executive-type man holding a glass of whiskey, with a half-empty bottle beside him on the table. And in block letters were the words "For Men of Distinction."

Motoring slowly through the Bowery section of New York City, we saw several samples of the finished product of the liquor industry's "men of distinction." One was sound asleep on the sidewalk, without shirt or shoes, beside him a broken chair from inside the flophouse, and an empty bottle nearby. A dozen or so others were sleeping or sitting or staggering or begging. We were told that indeed some of these had once been men of distinction—lawyers, doctors, professors, even ministers.

All of us have known men who were distinguished because of their accomplishments: men of wealth, men of fame, men of power, men of letters, men of talents, men of learning, men of abilities, men of affairs, etc. But Paul addressed Timothy as a "man of God" (1 Tim. 6:11). This is the highest title any man could seek, achieve, receive, or bestow. What a sublime honor for anyone to have the Apostle Paul thus address him!

Let us examine some of the characteristics that are common to all who are truly men of distinction.

1. *They live in one direction.* They have one motive, one aim, one goal, one ideal, one passion. All else is secondary to that one supreme purpose, whether it is money or holiness. Paul testified, "This one thing I do" (Phil. 3:13). But many others would have to admit, "These 40 things I dabble in."

I pastored a church in which two very contrasting men caught my attention. Both were good, honest, sincere, and capable. However, they were as different as night and day. One was always changing jobs, always learning a new trade, always moving around, yet never achieving for his family, his church, his God. The other man started at the bottom of an organization and stayed with it, working his way to the top. He was a pillar in the church and for many years had been respected and loved for miles around. He was a true man of distinction, living in one direction.

2. *They are guided by one principle.* "Step on people, if you must, to get ahead" was the way one young man framed his thesis. "Get it while you can" is the principle that shaped another's thinking. "I press toward the mark for the prize of the high calling of God in Christ Jesus" (Phil. 3:14) was the precept that kept the apostle steady.

They are guided by one principle—these men of distinction—whether they be men of the world or men of God. Their deepest motives are revealed in their daily actions, words, and thoughts. With Napoleon it was to conquer the world; with Lincoln it was truth and justice and righteousness; with Wesley it was holiness evangelism; with Schmelzenbach it was to light a candle in the darkness.

3. *They are predictable.* Napoleon was always fighting; Lincoln was always healing and uniting; Wesley was always preaching and writing and winning; Schmelzen-

bach was always loving and lifting. Men of distinction are always moving toward their goals. They are dependable. I have pastored men who were so regular in their attendance and so prompt in their arrival that I could set my watch by observing them step inside the church. If you are a man of God, it is easy to predict where you will be spending and investing your money and your time and talents. It will be easy to locate you at church time and at the appointed hour for witnessing in the homes.

4. *They are always trying to make converts.* I struck up a conversation with a man beside me on the plane and before I could tell him about Jesus, he was telling me about plastics. And before I could invite him to accept Christ, he was inviting me to quit the ministry and join him in the plastics industry! He was a man of distinction—perhaps more so than I! An unknown poet summed it up in these choice lines:

> *You talk about your riches,*
>   *Your stocks and bonds and gold;*
> *You talk about the weather,*
>   *Of days, some hot, some cold;*
> *But what of God's redemption,*
>   *And what of salvation's plan?*
> *Let's speak a word for Jesus,*
>   *And speak up like a man!*

5. *They become like their gods.* While every man becomes like the object of his worship, this is especially true of these men of distinction because they are by nature more intense and vigorous than most men. The man who worships at the shrine of the silver coin becomes covetous in his materialism. The man who worships the flesh becomes lustful and sensual. And the man who worships Jesus Christ becomes holy and clean and loving and zealous to win his neighbors to his Lord.

I like the scripture which says, "Enoch walked with God: and he was not; for God took him" (Gen. 5:24). A fairly short epitaph for a man who lived 365 years. But it speaks volumes. It tells us that Enoch and God became so well acquainted that they took long walks together. They had many things in common, for Enoch had become like the God he worshiped—and with whom he fellowshiped. It must have been late in the day when Enoch, seeing the setting sun, said, "Lord, I guess I had better be getting back home." And I think God must have said, "Enoch, why don't you go home with Me, because we are closer to My house than we are to yours." So Enoch went home with God.

Jesse Musick challenges us to be men of distinction by writing:

> The world today is looking for men who are not for sale—men who are honest from center to circumference, true to the heart's core; men with consciences as steady as the needle to the pole; men who will stand for the right if the heavens totter and the earth reels; men who can tell the truth and look the world right in the eye; men who will neither brag nor run; men who will neither flag nor flinch; men who can have courage without shouting it; men in whom the courage of everlasting life runs deep and strong; men who know their message and tell it; men who know their place and fill it; men who know their business and attend to it; men who will not lie, shirk nor dodge; men who are not too lazy to work—nor too proud to be poor.

Chapter 11

CONCEPTS
FOR SPIRITUAL LEADERS

A careful analysis will show us that spiritual leaders are motivated by certain concepts which other leaders do not necessarily possess. Let's examine some of these.

1. *Spiritual progress is a worthy goal.* Indeed this is the area where the highest success is demanded. If there be failure anywhere, it should not be in the spiritual realm. This goes not only for doctrinal, moral, and ethical principles, but it also applies to the advancement of God's work in the world. God's demands require our highest vision, our finest effort, our largest commitment, our keenest insight, and our strongest faith in His work. There can be no turning aside from the principle that God's work must grow. And grow it will if we who do His work are faithful in executing our responsibilities in a worthy way.

2. *Modern man is still hungry for the old-fashioned gospel.* Those who say that churches with high standards can never attract large crowds have forgotten that the largest churches in America today are churches with high standards, and that the modern-day cults make perhaps the greatest demands of all. Let us never yield to the temptation to blame any lack of progress on our high standards, our altar calls, our holiness doctrine. If some of

our churches are not growing, it is not because of these things. Sinful men and women are hungry and are seeking a way out of their sin, willing to pay the price for genuine salvation.

3. *It is normal for a spiritual church to grow.* If there is no growth, we have the right to ask, "Is it normal? Is it spiritual?" This is not to say that there will never be plateaus of consolidation covering a period of a few months. But if a church has not grown for two years or five years, it is time for us to ask some disturbing questions. Is our church a church in the truest sense of the word? Is it a normal church? Is it a spiritual church? Then why is it not growing?

The pastor needs to ask himself some very serious questions in his prayer closet on his knees before the open Bible. The church board members need to ask themselves some very pointed questions as they pray and ponder and study the work committed to them. The Sunday school teachers and officers need to ask themselves some perhaps embarrassing questions if their church is not growing. If you are a member of a church that is no larger than it was five years ago, why not ask yourself some personal questions about your part in the lack of growth in your church?

4. *It is possible for a growing church, even a large church, to still be a pure church.* On one occasion I met with a church board which had voted not to take in any more people into church membership because they said their church was already large enough. Their average attendance was 30. Their argument was that if they got to be a large church, they could not still be a spiritual church, a clean church, with good, solid, New Testament standards. But their concept was not accurate. Most of us have been in churches which were many times larger which were considered both spiritual and pure. As a matter of fact, Jesus had only 12 in His small group, and one of them turned out to be a traitor. Smallness is not always to be equated with purity.

5. *It is possible for a big church to still be friendly and keep the common touch.* It is doubtful if we can accurately state that the size of the church determines the friendliness of the people. One fine young couple was transferred to a new community and started attending a church of 50 people. They were present three Sundays and no one, including the pastor, even shook hands or spoke to them, although they waited around at the door to get acquainted. Other churches, running several hundred in attendance or even thousands in attendance, have organized themselves into small groups so that everyone is a part of a small, friendly family within the larger church family.

The New Testament Church was interested in numbers as well as souls. They kept an accurate account of the number of people in the Upper Room and counted the converts at Pentecost; they counted them again at least twice after Pentecost and on other occasions in the Early Church. Jesus was interested in quantity as well as quality. On many occasions the number attending His meetings were counted, and the record of that count is listed in the Bible.

I recall the story of the down-and-out sinner who attended a revival meeting for the first time and heard the preacher, as well as the people, speak of their burden for souls. When he left the church, no one had even spoken to him, so he said to the usher standing at the door, "I wish you people would forget all about souls and take an interest in me. I am lost." Although we should never worship at the shrine of statistics, yet we should be vitally interested in statistics, for statistics mean people. One layman summed it up this way: "We count people because people count."

6. *The gospel is worthy of our finest promotional efforts.* Why not promote the gospel? We promote toothpaste, beauty cream, and piston rings; why not promote the gospel of Jesus Christ? When men spend millions for promoting things for personal gain, then why should Christians be ashamed to spend time and effort in promoting the gospel for the sake of a hungry, dying world? If salesmen can be challenged and trained and inspired—even pressured—to sell more insurance, should Christians draw back when challenged to win souls for Jesus Christ?

A motto on a desk in an office in New York City reads, "The whole world to win." The man behind that motto and that desk is a Communist. He is not content to win just a few here and there. He is not content just to win New York City or the Eastern seaboard or the United States. He is out to win the world and he is not ashamed of it. He is promoting everything he can promote in order to spread the evil doctrine of Communism.

We who call ourselves Christians have a world to win too. Are we ashamed to promote this fact? Do we object to getting mail from headquarters prodding us to action? Are we reluctant to put on Sunday school contests, to nail up posters, to teach training classes, to go after prospects and knock on doors? The goal is that the church may grow and that souls may be saved before it is everlastingly too late. The gospel is worth promoting! Let's promote it. And the church is worth promoting. Let's do it without apology!

Chapter 12

SEARCH FOR EXCELLENCE

Quality saints are an imperative need in every local congregation if the kingdom of God is to be advanced in God's way in our time. Undoubtedly these people of high caliber exist in every local congregation, but perhaps, in many cases, in potential only. This seems to say that we must put on a search for excellence to develop leadership in every church. Peter Drucker, in *The Practice of Management,* described leadership in this manner:

> Leadership is not magnetic personality—that can just as well be demagoguery. It is not making friends and influencing people—that is salesmanship. Leadership is the lifting of a man's vision to higher sights—the raising of a man's performance to a high standard—the building of a man's personality beyond its normal limitations.[1]

Mr. Drucker has also stated that management is mobilizing human effectiveness. The purpose of organization, he says, is to make common men do uncommon things. Thus we must conclude that many men have potential for greater effectiveness than is now seen on the surface. In considering this search for excellence, I am referring closely to some notes from a lecture to preachers by Harold T. Jackson of Canton, Ohio.

1. *Generate confidence.* Excellence always improves when men are challenged to believe in themselves, to believe in their work, believe in their methods, and to be inspired in their highest achievements. Morale is always a large factor in challenging men to do their best for God and the Kingdom.

2. *Inspire a determination to excel.* The word *excellence* comes from the same root as *excel,* meaning "to accomplish, achieve, do more, be better, be superior." The building of quality saints suggests the building of a high determination to accomplish for God.

3. *Develop trained subordinates.* Perhaps in no area is the church lacking so much as in the area of training for leadership and churchmanship within the ranks of church members. Kingdom purposes can be achieved only when men are trained to achieve them. If it is important for doctors and teachers to train their subordinates, it is more important for church leaders to train new leaders to advance God's work.

4. *Challenge each person to his maximum potential.* Those who teach in the lower grades of the public school system will tell you it is important to challenge a child to his maximum potential. They also tell us that each child is challenged at a different point and at a different level. This may explain why some children are bored while others are simply confused.

Perhaps we could learn in the church from this procedure. Each layman in the church must be challenged to his maximum potential in leadership and service. To do this, we must carefully evaluate the potential of each person in the area of his interest and talents and then challenge him to prepare himself for greater service. All of us have known church members who quit the church because they felt they were wasting their time. There was simply nothing for them to do. They were never assigned a responsibility so they went where they could be put to work and be made useful. We must learn how to challenge our people in Christian service.

5. *Respond to provocation dispassionately and objectively.* Leaders must be trained to "take it on the chin." They must be trained and taught to be creative about their problems. They must be inspired to take criticism objectively, without becoming critical. The way a person responds to provocation under pressure is indicative of his ability as a leader. However, even in this area, people can be trained and taught to improve themselves by self-discipline.

6. *Have a dynamic approach to new ideas.* We are living in times that demand constant change in the church. Methods, programs, and equipment that were in vogue 20 years ago may have already lived out their usefulness. While the gospel emphasis does not change, yet the manner in which that emphasis is presented must change. The church must keep in step with the times or it will not survive. Do not fear innovative people in the church. They could be your best asset. The church must keep in step with changing times or it will be shaken apart by future shock which is already upon us.

7. *Enable others to gain recognition for their achievements.* Quality leaders are always eager to give credit where credit is due. God pity the man who wants all the credit for what other people do, for he is thus indicating his spiritual poverty. The man who can sincerely brag on the accomplishments and achievements of other people, even his competitors, is a big man.

8. *Move consistently toward goals.* Of course this presupposes that there will be goals in the first place: short and long-ranged. In order to know how one is progressing in the direction of his goals, he needs a chart, a graph, a list of figures, a set of statistics, or other measurements

94

whereby he can spot his accomplishments. Once goals are set and accepted, every effort must be made to achieve them. All must be informed of progress in this direction.

9. ***Develop eagerness to pay the price for accomplishment.*** God's people need to be motivated just as the employees of General Motors or General Electric need to be motivated. While the basis of motivation may be different, the outcome should be similar—accomplishment. However, those who pay the price for accomplishment in the church may find the price tag greater than in the secular world.

10. ***Maintain a high level of thrust in all serious endeavors.*** It is not enough to get started in God's work. It is not enough to put on a brief spurt of progress in spiritual things. There must always be the steady follow-through after the excitement of the beginning has passed. Quality saints need to understand that there is a great need for serious, mature, constant labor even when the glamor of it has passed.

At this point, true excellence is always discovered. The man who can follow through his assignments without recognition, remuneration, and even large results at times, is the mature man. Thank God for the large group of substantial people who pay their tithe, attend prayer meeting, make calls, sacrifice, teach classes, and serve in obscure places even when results are not forthcoming. These are the salt of the church.

Chapter 13

HOW LEADERSHIP SHOWS THROUGH

Peter Drucker states that "management involves the coordination of human and material resources toward objective accomplishment." Four basic elements in management are wrapped up in this statement:

1. Toward objective
2. Through people
3. Via techniques
4. In an organization

Let us consider how leadership shows through in the local church as related to both ministerial and lay leadership.

1. *What the leader is.* The leader is loyal, fair, and democratic. He is not a bulldozer nor a steamroller nor a whip-cracker nor an authoritarian person. He works with people. He is gracious even when he does not get his own way. He is kind to those who are subordinate to him even when they blunder. A leader is composed even when the pressure is on. He is emotionally stable at all times. A leader is courageous and willing to get off the fence and be counted.

He is careful to spell out directions and job descriptions. A leader is able to say, "I am wrong," when he blunders. He never alibis his way out of situations. He never blames others for his own failures. He assumes his own responsibilities willingly and gladly. A leader may differ with people, but he does not spend his time fussing with them. If people go from his presence weeping because of conflict with him, or if they resign in large numbers because they cannot work with him, then the leader needs to examine himself, his motives, his heart, his methods, and change his procedures.

2. *What a leader has.* A leader has finesse. He knows there is an art to leadership and he seeks to discover it. He employs executive etiquette in his dealings with people. He learns to be fair in handling difficult situations. He learns to work his way through problems without having battles. He finds ways to bring people together rather than pit them against each other. A leader has vision. He sees ahead. He sees farther ahead than other men or he would not be a leader. He imparts this vision to other people who are laboring with him. Because of his leadership ability, they too catch the vision and seek to help him achieve his goals.

A leader has vigor. There is no place in God's work for anemic leadership. Halfhearted, careless preparation always shows through in results achieved. A leader never goes into his meetings in a careless manner. Courage and vitality are an essential part of his nature. A leader has insight. He is able to unfold problems and look into them and see where the trouble lies. He knows human nature well enough to be able to guide his program through a variety of personalities. He has perception enough to know what can be accomplished and what cannot be accomplished. He is aware of the consequences of his proposals and of his choices.

3. *What the leader knows.* He knows his people and his work. He is a student of human nature and of the work in which he is engaged. He knows how individual people

will react to individual proposals. The leader knows how to organize himself and organize his work. He disciplines himself to meet deadlines and he teaches others to do the same. He is prompt, always arriving ahead of time, always starting on time, always closing on time. He prepares agendas for his meetings and he distributes them before the meeting begins. He prepares adequate materials to spell out the details of the program which he has in mind.

A leader knows where he is going and he knows how to get there. He has personal goals ahead of himself and he has plans to reach those goals. He knows what he wishes to accomplish at any given board meeting or committee meeting and he has plans and methods to accomplish the business proposed. A leader knows where his people ought to go and he knows how to get them there. A man of vision, he can foresee what ought to be done and he formulates plans to reach his objectives. He does not go into a meeting unprepared and without plans.

4. *What a leader does.* A leader communicates. He talks it out with people. He learns how to get the message through. He uses every means to accomplish this, such as: charts, graphs, blackboards, mimeographed items, individual contacts, and public presentations. A leader cooperates even when he does not get his own way. If he is outvoted, he joins the majority without rancor and complaining. He does not show hurt feelings even when he feels them. He never goes around complaining to other people because he was outvoted in the board meeting.

A leader also delegates responsibility and authority to other people because he knows he cannot do all the work by himself. He does this because he knows that other people can do it as well or perhaps even better than he. He does this because he also knows other people need to be involved in the business and in the work in which they are engaged. A leader informs. He lets people know what is happening. He keeps them well advised on financial matters, all plans and programs, all action, all reports, all activities, and all dates. He understands that spiritual people make the best choices when they have all the facts at hand. So he gives them these facts.

5. *How a leader acts.* A leader sees the big picture and displays his own bigness in showing this big picture to others. He does not lord it over other people but joins them in exploring what God has challenged them to do. A leader helps his people set their own goals. He does not impose goals on those with whom he labors. He helps them set their own goals. Nor does he chide them or become impatient with them when their goals are not the goals which he would have chosen for them. He shows his people how to arrive at reasonable goals and then advertises and helps people to reach those goals. He acts with sympathy when people fail to reach goals but also honors those who reach theirs.

A leader takes pride in his own work as a leader. He seeks to be the most efficient leader that he can be. He studies books on leadership and motivation. By precept and by example, he challenges others to a higher plane of effectiveness and usefulness in their leadership. A leader acts like a leader. He looks like a leader. He thinks like a leader. He has the bearing and the carriage of a leader. He has the confidence and the humility of a leader. He surrounds himself with others who are also leaders in the making.

Chapter 14

TOOLS FOR PROBLEM SOLVERS

In *The Art of Decision Making,* Joseph D. Cooper describes some of the tools that a problem solver uses in business circles. Using these as a basis, let us expand the ideas and apply them to areas of the spiritual realm.

1. *A broad general background.* If a person is to effectively solve a problem that may confront him, he will need to know more than the problem itself. He needs a broad base of information and education on many subjects. This can be achieved not only through formal education but also through constant reading. Indeed the man who quits studying when he gets out of school is not equipped to be a problem solver. For this reason it is imperative that those who work in church circles read widely and constantly, studying always to improve themselves.

2. *Adequate technical background.* The day of the specialist is upon us. As surely as doctors and lawyers and teachers and mechanics specialize in definite areas, so must the man who works in God's kingdom specialize in problems that confront the church. He needs to know all there is to know about the operation of the church. If he is working in Sunday school, he needs to know everything

about the operation of the Sunday school. The same is true of the youth organization, the missionary program, the administrative affairs of the church, and other areas.

3. *Institutional awareness.* If we are to properly solve problems in the local church, we need to be informed regarding the church *Manual,* the local program, and the previous planning of the church activities. Problems must always be solved in the light of our total commitment as a denomination and as a local church. We must also keep in mind that some things which confront us are beyond debate.

4. *Self-organization.* The man who would be a problem solver is himself an organized person. He has learned to solve his own problems and he has learned to help others solve their problems. How can an undisciplined person be expected to tell others how to discipline themselves? How can a person know how to solve the problems of the church when he cannot solve his own problems? Problem solving begins at home with one's self.

5. *Resource utilization.* The problem solver gets all the help that is available and applies it to the problems at hand. This would indicate that an abundance of preparation is necessary before conclusions are reached. The problem solver must know all about the problem. He must know all about the people involved in the problem. He must understand the mechanics of the problem. He must understand why the problem occurred and how he can go about finding a solution. He must understand the ramifications in arriving at a solution.

6. *Communication skills.* It goes without saying that the problem solver must be a master at communication. He must be able to get his thoughts across as well as receive the thoughts expressed by others. He must be able to understand what people are saying and even what they are thinking. He must learn to master the fine art of reading character and perceiving thought. He must not only be able to arrive at a conclusion which will satisfactorily solve the problem, but he must be able to get others to see and accept his point of view. Thus the problem solver must be a good salesman.

7. *Interpersonal proficiency.* The problem solver must know how to get along well with people. His aim is not only to communicate, but to get people to accept what he is saying. The problem solver must get his ideas across in the manner that will cause people to want to accept them and put them into practice. This automatically eliminates the bulldozing, the whip-cracking, the domineering approach. The problem solver knows how to create a team spirit and get support for the ideas which he presents.

8. *Action personality.* The problem solver is a man who is alive, alert, and eager. He cannot have a casual approach to the problem nor the solution. He must remember that action on his part inspires action on the part of others. Therefore, he must be a man highly motivated to find the solution, to sell it, and put it into practice. He uses this personality skill not for selfish gain or advantage but that the problem may be resolved. His goal, therefore, is not self-glorification, but problem solving.

Chapter 15

PROFILE OF
A TROUBLESHOOTER

Moses, Elijah, David. Different men for different ages. Each of them, sandwiched into crucial periods of history, cast lengthening shadows on men and events. Each of them had unique abilities. But each of them had one particular common problem or challenge: how to continually accomplish God's purposes within the framework of day-by-day testing, trial, and temptation. Each man faced different problems, just as you and I. But each faced a common need: They had to know how to proceed effectively in the directing of God's people.

Just as we, today, need the assistance of others, so did they. They had to have outside help—someone who could view them and their problems from another perspective. They needed a troubleshooter. God provided the balm of His Spirit under a juniper tree for Elijah. He gave Nathan to David. And for Moses He provided his father-in-law, Jethro.

Jethro, though not remembered in the same manner as the great Lawgiver, nonetheless brought Moses through a vital stage in his life. God gave this priest of the Midianites to Moses when his mental and physical strength was taxed. And because Moses was tired and awed at the size of his assignment, he needed help in defining his objectives, his alternatives, his course of action. Such a great man as Moses in need? Of course! Great men are always in need. And their strength is in knowing it, in finding a source of help, and accepting the help when it becomes available.

Jethro had some suggestions which are as useful for us as they were lifesaving for Moses. In Exodus 18 we find the setting in which Moses labored and a profile of Jethro, the man who helped Moses spot trouble and solve it. Jethro offered 12 tests for problem solving.

1. *The test of observation* (v. 13). While Moses, Jethro, and Aaron sat down to eat a sacrificial meal before God, they recounted the mercy of the Lord in delivering them from Pharaoh. In Moses' tent that evening, Jethro could see the weariness etched on the leader's face. The next morning, as usual, Moses sat in judgment before long lines of people who came with both petty and serious matters. Jethro observed the strain upon Moses. Quite logically, he suggested a simple plan, devised to disperse some of the authority without separating the power from Moses.

Some say that Moses should have seen the problem himself. However, he was too close to it. He feared dissension, he saw long lines of waiting people, and he had to work fast. But he was too close to the forest to see the trees. He was not aware of the self-imposed danger, nor that good men who could have helped were standing idle. Jethro observed, studied, offered a solution. It gave Moses the "break" he needed.

2. *The test of recognition* (v. 14). Jethro found strength for Moses by identifying the problem. Moses, however, was so preoccupied with trying to settle problems that he had little time to see *the* problem, which was that he was being overwhelmed. Briefly, Jethro helped Moses to see the scope of his role. Moses was the lone chief justice

104

on a type of Supreme Court with no lower courts at all. But he never thought of it that way; moreover, he reasoned that it was *his* duty to handle each case. Both the scope and the weight of the problem were so great that he had little time for reflection. One of the earliest targets for trouble shooters must be that of recognizing, defining, and weighing the problem that exists.

3. *The test of isolation* (v. 14). Another key Jethro found was to isolate the problem from the others Moses faced. Problems? Moses had them. But Jethro centered on an important one: "Why are you trying to do all *this* alone?" Until we can separate one problem from the next, not much relief will be found.

In a sense many problems are related to others. But isolating the one we wish to deal with, centering our thoughts upon it alone, will save us from the entanglement of overextension into other perils, both real and imaginary.

4. *The test of inquiry* (v. 14). Good trouble shooters are full of sound, reasonable questions. No need for asking the "unanswerable whys." But there is need, after spotting the problem, to probe, looking for soft spots, weaknesses, and strengths. One must locate hidden meanings, gather information, marshal all the facts. Had Moses begun this way, his time, effort, energy, and ability would have been spared undue stress. "Why *am* I doing this particular job?" is one of the healthiest questions one might ask himself. If another could do it as well and release me for other duties, why shouldn't he? Moses had fallen into the trap of taking on more work for himself than was necessary. A little inquiry at the outset would have averted the situation.

But the *right* kind of inquiry does not involve a foolhardy brand of curiosity. This bit of verse speaks volumes:

> *Willie was a good boy,*
>   *But Willie is no more;*
> *What Willie thought was H_2O*
>   *Was H_2SO_4* (sulphuric acid).

All serious inquiry involves an examination of purpose and an amassing of the necessary factual material.

5. *The test of ventilation* (vv. 15-16). Part of the wisdom of Jethro was in letting Moses answer the question put to him. Good troubleshooters don't always have to answer their own questions. Jethro let Moses do the talking. Ventilation of the problem and setting forth possible solutions, good and bad, is basic to problem solving. The more the problem is opened up, the more likely are the solutions to be seen. Gathered opinions, straw ballots, brainstorming are all successful tools for the troubleshooter. While it is possible that a law of diminishing returns could result in gathering more solutions than are needed, the vital test of ventilation is in separating the chaff from the wheat.

6. *The test of analysis* (vv. 17-18). Jethro helped Moses to see the end result at the beginning of his plight. Together they analyzed the problem. They made a target of the trouble. They gauged each facet and reexamined the peril before them. In the context of these verses, Jethro sounded a warning. Then, blow upon blow, the factual evidence he presented sustained his reasoning power. Jethro was a ballast, a catalyst for weary Moses. He proved to his son-in-law that foresight *is* better than hindsight. Moses was saved a great deal of heartache by Jethro's close analysis.

7. *The test of alternatives* (vv. 19-20). The strength of good leadership ability lies in knowing what options are available. While selection of the *correct* solution comes in testing all alternatives, Jethro and Moses found it advisable to study present methods as well as untried ideas.

Obviously, in testing alternatives you must surrender to the fact that the one you pick could turn out to be less desirable than expected. A willingness to fail, not the surrender to failure, is the risk that must be taken. How many ways can the problem be handled? What are the likely solutions? So that all alternatives are before you, list even those obviously less worthy than others. Getting alternatives out in the open enables a leader to determine his options.

8. *The test of testing* (vv. 21-23). Solutions cannot be found unless you test the alternatives open to you. What will be the consequences of each action taken? Is it worth the risk? What *are* the risks? What will happen if you do nothing? What is the best possible solution? How could you prove it? What tools do you possess which could be used as a gauge in determining potential results? Are you willing to stick with one solution and give it a fair try once you believe in it?

Once you know your alternatives, testing is a matter of elimination. By a process of measuring strengths, weaknesses, and reactions, you will be able to do two things: *(a)* conserve your energy for more important items, and *(b)* concentrate your effort and energy on what is vital. It may be that alternatives once thought essential will, after testing, prove ineffective. And if your testing has been both fair and rigorous, other plans will come to the surface. Thus you continue the conquest of exploration, which, in itself, is the basis for troubleshooting.

9. *The test of motivation* (v. 23). "What will other people think?" is, unfortunately, a greatly discredited view today. What people feel, think, believe, surmise *is* most crucial to the success of any problem solving. Credibility is at the heart of motivation. If the people following a leader do not believe in what he says, is, or does, why should they follow? The reaction and acceptance of co-laborers, superiors, subordinates, and common people hinge upon a leader's ability to make people *believe* in what he says, what he does, what he *is*. If this cannot be done, they will not follow or be motivated for long. Part of the key for Moses was seeing Jethro's advice of *sharing* the burden with other people. When *they* had something at stake in the solution of day-to-day events, they were motivated. And with Jethro's help, Moses magnified the solution more than the problem.

Does it motivate you when people around you threaten, complain, and entwine themselves and others around the problem? Of course not! Are you encouraged to take heart, find solutions, and continue in the work when superiors or others prod you with the "unsolvable" problem? Not on your life! Not only was Moses discouraged, so were his people. But once they saw that the solution was working, they got excited about its value. They were sold on the possibilities *within* them, not on the plight around them! That's motivation. It must be made alive! It must be graphically explainable! It must be believable! Moses learned one essential lesson in motivation from Jethro: People are motivated by possibilities, not problems! It is no less true in your church today!

10. *The test of implementation* (vv. 24-25). Moses wasn't just standing there; he was busy. The wise counsel of Jethro lifted much of his old work load, but this freed him for more significant tasks. Jethro helped Moses in many ways, but implementation of management planning was one of the best. Both of them developed a philosophy of troubleshooting which can be used today. It is this: A man should work smarter, not necessarily harder. The Lawgiver was a hard worker, evidenced in his leadership years prior to Jethro's visit in his tent that night. But wiser planning enabled him to use his time in other more needed areas, lessened his own physical and mental stress as well

as that of his people, and thereby brought peace and harmony within the camp.

Implementation puts a plan into action. For Moses, and for us, the sooner we get on with things that are essential, the better. Andrew Carnegie once said, "It marks a big step in a man's development when he comes to realize that other men can be called in to help him do a better job than he can do alone."

11. *The test of conservation* (v. 26). The reward of troubleshooting comes when you've hit the problem head-on and the once insoluble threat begins to dissolve. If proper procedure has been followed, you may rest in the assurance that some of the answers will come quickly. Some may follow more slowly, but they will come. Once Moses got the machinery in fine running condition, he kept it that way. Possibly there were some who didn't like it. They wanted things "like they used to be." The personal accessibility to Moses was gone, but Moses was a better equipped leader, more refreshed for weightier matters.

To slip back into the old ruts and not do some troubleshooting occasionally is bad for churches in the human-relations sense, and individual Christians in the spiritual sense. It is a changing world presenting new problems constantly which demand new solutions if there is to be survival, let alone progress.

12. *The test of satisfaction* (v. 27). Moses was on target. There is nothing quite as satisfying as that. And because he was, his people were. This lesson taught by Jethro was no quickie course on "Ten Easy Steps to Successful Human Relations in the Desert." It was an in-depth, introspective type of look into the soul of a harassed leader. The greatest lesson, possibly, that Moses had to learn was that even leaders are men in need of help. And he learned it well. Satisfaction came. His mission was accomplished.

Jethro was able to continue on his way. God had him in the right place at the right time. Because of this, Moses was now prepared to go up into the mountain. There his feet were to stand on holy ground and he would receive the commandments of the Lord. He went with the certainty in his own soul that God was directing him.

Chapter 16

ON LEARNING
TO COPE WITH PROBLEMS

In learning to cope with problems, I am reminded of the philosophy of a district superintendent in the early days of our denomination who had this to say about pastors who wrote him about their problems:

> I do not rush to their help. In fact, often I do not even answer their letters when they ask me about solutions to problems because I am convinced that one-third of the problems can be solved by the pastor without me, and one-third of the problems will solve themselves in the course of time, and one-third of the problems cannot be solved by me nor the pastor nor God himself.

I am sure that if he were living today he would look for a more scientific approach to the solving of problems in the church. The complexity of our problems today demand it.

Once again, I am indebted to Joseph D. Cooper *(The Art of Decision Making)* for many of the ideas below.

1. *Looking at the problem.* The problem should be stated clearly and written down, concisely and briefly. Then it is a good idea to ask yourself, "Is the stated problem the *real* problem?" If it is not, then look deeper until you find the real problem at hand and define it. Also, you should ask, "Is the problem clearly understood? Do all of

those involved in the solution of the problem understand exactly what the problem is and what it involves?"

Then you should ask yourself if you are the right person to consider the problem. Is it your problem, or does it belong to someone else? Also check the timing. Is this the correct time to find the solution? Has the time gone by or has it not yet arrived? Be sure to approach the problem with an open mind. Solutions cannot be achieved unless the approach is objective.

2. *Looking behind the problem.* The problem solver must understand the background of the problem. He will want to know what triggered the problem in the first place. He will want to amass and assimilate all the facts relating to the cause of the problem. Thus he will enable himself to make a fair evaluation of the problem. This may involve personal research but will also call for advice from other people. Thus the man who is to tackle the problem will find handles and soft spots.

3. *Looking around the problem.* Answers must be found to these questions: How is the problem related to your goals? How does the problem affect the plans that you have outlined? At what point does the problem touch the policies that have been set forth? What is the probable consequence of even considering the problem? Do you hope for a one-time solution, or is this a problem which will continue or recur with apparently no permanent solution? The answers to these questions will give much-needed insight.

4. *Looking beyond the problem.* Questions to be considered here are: Who will make the ultimate decision regarding the solution? Will that decision be made by one person, by a committee, by a board, or by a congregational vote? Who will spell out the decision once it has been made? Then, how should the final decision be presented? Should it simply be announced and let drop? Should it be presented in the form of a mimeographed sheet or a

112

brochure? Does the final decision call for graphs, charts, statistics, directives, prohibitions, other items?

Consideration should also be given to the person or persons to be affected by this decision. How many people will be affected? In what way?

Finally, how will the decision be implemented? How far-reaching is this decision? Will the "cure be worse than the disease"? What other critical factors may be affected?

5. *Looking into the problem.* Up to this point you have been walking around the problem and prodding it much as a farmer would walk around a laystack and prod it with his pitchfork, looking for some hidden object within it. Now you are ready to start digging in. The first step is mapping the problem—breaking it down into sections. Some problems present highly complicated difficulties that cannot be easily segregated. Other problems are more simple.

It will be helpful to consider any previous experience relating to this area. Has anyone gone through this problem or similar problems before? Is there a precedent? How has this problem been tackled in other days or by other people? And with what results? Again, what are the opinions of the experts in this area? Where are the danger points? Where are the hidden rocks, and how can you locate them so that you can steer clear of them?

6. *Looking at the facts related to the problem.* What salient information is available to you? Can you lay hold of that information? Have you disciplined yourself to study all of the facets of the problem? What has your study revealed to you? What are some of the ramifications which have surfaced? Have you followed these leads to discover what is involved? What related information is available to you regarding the problem? When the facts are known, rank them in order of importance and carefully examine your options.

7. *Looking into the choices that the problem presents.* Now that you have looked at all the facts of the problem, weigh them. What are the choices before you as you seek solutions? It would be well for you to jot down various solutions available and rank them in order of importance. Are there compromises that could or should be made? What are the consequences?

The next step is to integrate the total picture. You have prodded the problem from every direction; you have conducted an in-depth study; you have examined all the facts and considered all the choices and consequences; and now you come to the moment of decision. If there are two or more possible solutions to the problem, you must adopt one and discard the other. You have already admitted the possibility of repercussions to your chosen line of action, so brace yourself for whatever may happen. The decision may have to be made by one person, sometimes by a vote of the committee, board, or congregation, but usually the moment for decision making is a serious and lonely moment.

8. *Looking at the solution instead of the problem.* Now that you have come to a decision, it is time for you to spell out that decision for all to know. This must be done carefully, prayerfully, and in detail. It is not always possible for all of the facts and all of the steps to be announced at once, but basic information should be released. This could be in the form of a mimeographed sheet announcing what the decision is, who was involved in making the decision, who is to carry out the decision, how the solution will be applied, what new action or changes must take place, the effective date for this to be done, and other pertinent information.

Selling the solution to all people concerned is a vital part in problem solving. Again, it is important to remember that the best-informed people make the best decisions. If your people are given the facts related to the decision, this will help to keep the problem solved. When problems crop up again, it is usually because the people involved have not been adequately informed nor sold on the solution. It is also well to remember that the timing of the announcement is important. There is always action and reaction at this point. Hopefully, the people involved will be motivated to look ahead and not look back. Most problem solving will bring rewarding results if adequate care and preparation is made in discovering and implementing the solution.

Chapter 17

HOW TO PICK A WINNER

Jesus was both an Administrator and an Organizer. He believed in the modern principles of spiritual leadership. Although it could be argued that of the 12 men which He chose to be His apostles one of them was a loser instead of a winner, it must also be remembered that there were other factors entering into such a choice, including the fulfilling of scripture. (From the human viewpoint, it could be observed that Jesus had a better batting average on picking men than most!) But His association with these men for three and one-half years plus the power of Pentecost changed these ordinary men into extraordinary personalities. In selecting leadership, lay or ministerial, for whatever position in the church, it would be well to ask the following 10 questions about the person under consideration.

1. *Is he a spiritual person?* Not a legalist, not a liberal, not a fanatic, not lopsided. Is he simply a spiritual man? Is he faithful in attendance? Does he tithe regularly and give offerings beyond his tithe? Does he read his Bible and pray consistently? Does he have solid convictions and stand by them? Is he a growing Christian?

2. *Is he dependable?* Does he arrive at church on time every time? Is he well prepared in advance of his arrival? Is he honest in all his dealings with his fellowman? Is he thrifty in regard to spending his money? Is he open and approachable, easy to communicate with? Can you count on him to be present at every service, including Sunday evening, prayer meeting, revival services, missionary meetings, and business meetings of all kinds? Does he take his responsibilities seriously when given an assignment?

3. *Is he willing to work?* Does he hold a steady job? How many different kinds of jobs has he had in the last five years? Is he able to motivate himself to do his work or does he need to be prodded into doing what he is assigned to do? Does he meet deadlines? Does he get his work done on time? Nothing nullifies leadership so much as laziness.

4. *Is he loyal?* Is he loyal to the *Manual?* Does he stand by the rules of the church? Does he support the doctrines of the church? Is he in sympathy with the standards of the church? Does he operate in accordance with the guidelines set forth in the *Manual* of the church? Is he loyal to leadership? Is he dependable when it comes to standing by his superiors? Can they count on him, or is he likely to knife them in the back? Is he loyal to the program of the church? Does he believe 100 percent in the mission of the church and in its methods of operation? Will he support the financial obligations of the church and endorse the paying of budgets to various causes, such as missions and education? Loyalty is a must in picking a winner.

5. *Does he have good judgment?* Does his common sense show through in all that he does? Are his decisions sound? Can you count on him to do the right thing at the right time without being constantly instructed in every detail? Can he keep confidences or is he gossipy, spilling forth everything that he hears?

6. *Does he get along well with people?* Is he a good mixer? Or does he rub people the wrong way? Does he know how to communicate with ease? Is he domineering or is he excessively timid? Is he the kind of man who will pull people together or pull them apart? Does he create good human relations for himself and for the church?

7. *Is he optimistic?* Does he have a positive outlook on life? Or is he always negative, always critical? Is he a complainer and a faultfinder or is he a confidence builder? Is he frequently saying unkind or uncomplimentary things about people or about the church or does he seem to be able to find something good to say about somebody or something? Does he have a gloomy personality or is he bright and cheerful? Are people attracted or repelled by him?

8. *Does he have a good record up to now?* What growth has he shown in his assignment? Is he productive? What is his record of achievement up to the present time? What do his superiors at work think of him? Have they found that he is dependable enough to take the initiative and to work diligently without having someone stand over him? Would he be sadly missed if he were to resign his present job?

9. *Does he behave well under stress?* How does he act when the pressure is on and the tide turns against him? Does he go to pieces under criticism? Does he fight back or does he honestly examine himself to see if he is conducting himself as he should? Does he get discouraged easily when people do not brag on him? Does he often feel that he is not appreciated? Is he a quitter when he does not get his own way? Does he buckle when the pressure is on or when people disagree with him?

10. *Does he motivate other people?* Are other people

around challenged to do better because he is present or are they demoralized when he is around? Does he strengthen the morale of the organization or does he weaken it? Does he have a good team spirit or is he a lone wolf? Does he make friends easily or is he difficult to befriend? Is he a booster or a knocker? A builder or a wrecker?

PART THREE

THE POSTURE OF AN ACHIEVER

I can do all things through Christ which strengtheneth me.
—PHIL. 4:13

Chapter 18

THE GRASSHOPPER COMPLEX

When I was a boy, I considered Alejandro to be the greatest cattleman in the whole country. Perhaps I was awed by him because he was raised on Kings' Ranch and because he knew all the tricks of the trade in dealing with cattle. He could diagnose and cure a sick animal with amazing accuracy. He was an expert at branding, roping, and dehorning. He knew each of our 200 cows by name or by number and loved them every one.

This amazing man professed one insight, however, which disturbed me a little as a lad: All his predictions and actions were based on the phases of the moon. For instance, he would say to me, "All of the calves being born for the next three days will be heifers." Later his prediction would change in the other direction, and I must admit that he was right at least half of the time. He also planted his garden and his crops according to the light of the moon. He even predicted the first frosts by that. I respected his overall judgment so thoroughly that I hardly questioned his pronouncements even regarding the phases of the moon.

Tying on to Alejandro's theories, I have concluded in more recent years that some people must have been born in the dark of the moon. My conclusions are based on their negative personality traits. They are perennial pessimists, always looking on the dark side of things, always negative in their outlook, always against every proposition which is presented. Evidently this twist of human personality is not straightened out by the grace of God, for often we discover that some of the finest Christians are negative—legalistic, ultraconservative, and opposed to every new idea presented. I believe that on the average there is at least one "abominable no-man" on every church board.

Let us listen to what some of his suggestions are when new ideas for progress are presented.

1. *We do not have the money.* This is the usual beginning point. Perhaps it is because money is so important in his own thinking. Perhaps it is because he always pays cash for what he buys, whether it be a new home or a new car or a new farm, and thus demands that the church do the same. Or on the contrary, it may be that he has such small financial resources himself that he believes that the church also is in poverty. So he automatically complains that the church debt is already too big, that the church budgets are getting larger every year, the pastor's salary is already too high, there is a recession coming or inflation is upon us, or local working conditions are not what they ought to be. Money is often a sore spot with negative thinkers.

2. *This proposal is too modern for us.* Or sometimes they say, "It is too old-fashioned." One reason is about as good as another reason when a person doesn't want to do something.

3. *Let's take a while to pray about it.* This is usually the curse of death pronounced from spiritual lips. The man who advocates this often does so in the hope that the proposal will die before the next board meeting, or that he will have time to put on a "spiritual" campaign against it. Coupled with this same idea is the thought that "We are

not ready for this yet," or, "This is not the time to do it."

4. *Let's appoint a committee.* This is a graceful way to kill almost any project, for often the committee is not appointed, is not instructed, or never meets, and the whole idea is forgotten.

This abominable no-man has an excuse and an alibi for every failure in the church. Here are some of his time-worn so-called reasons for spiritual stagnation in the church, some of which are suggested by Bennett Dudney in his book on church growth.

1. *Our standards are too high.* People would rather belong to a church where they can smoke and drink and go to shows instead of joining our church which prohibits all of these. If we would just lower our standards a little bit, we could double our membership.

2. *Our methods hold us back.* No one wants to go down to the altar and make a spectacle of himself in the presence of the entire congregation. If people could just sign a card and shake hands with the preacher, that should be enough, for conversion is a matter of the heart anyway.

3. *Our community will not accept our message.* Everyone here is either Catholic or Baptist. This is a hard place. Preachers come and preachers go, and we have heard all of them. This place is burned-over territory.

4. *Our building is inadequate.* It is either too small or too large or too old or too hard to heat. Therefore, people will not come under these circumstances. Our location is not good. The community is too poor or too rich or too far out in the country or too hard to find or too near the inner city or is surrounded by an ethnic neighborhood. Therefore, this place is hopeless. Alibis and excuses are available to anyone who wishes to use them, and the man with the grasshopper complex is sure to find an abundance of them or else manufacture some of his own.

Those who are pessimistic in their outlook usually refer back to the "good old days" of the past. Here are a few of their favorite thoughts.

1. In the good old days we used to have three-Sunday revivals and protracted meetings and fill the house and fill the altar every night. What is the matter with us now? Aren't we spiritual anymore? Back in those days people got blessed and shouted and climbed the tent poles. And we didn't have hypocrites either. Now we are so calm and so quiet that I am afraid some people among us are not living right.

2. In the good old days we had a preacher who ran the aisles and shouted and jumped through a loop he made with his hands. He was really spiritual. We don't see much of this today. We worry too much about education. All this money for training preachers is wasted because it ruins them. If the Lord should call me to preach, I would just open my mouth and let God fill it.

3. In the good old days people got blessed and gave as the Lord directed. I am tired of all of this talk about tithing. I can remember when we paid our pastor only $10.00 a week. Now we pay him $150 per week plus all those extras. Now we have big budgets but in those days we didn't have any budgets at all.

4. In the good old days we had a pastor who called on us every Tuesday morning and stayed for dinner and for most of the afternoon. Now we are lucky to get our pastor to call on us twice a year. Why all this talk about personal work and surveying and calling? We pay our pastor to do that, and he is always trying to get somebody else to do his work for him.

5. In the good old days we just went to a vacant lot, pitched a tent, had a revival, organized a church, and worshipped in a store building. Now we are so nice that we have to pay out big money for a nice building and a

parsonage and an educated pastor before we can get a church started. Is this necessary? Haven't we forgotten the romance of the ministry?

Well, there you have it. A picture of the "good old days" psychology. I have personally heard each one of the above ideas presented in church board meetings. I also am old enough to have lived in the "good old days" and will have to admit that there is half-truth in some of the statements. But there is also half-untruth in these statements. The "good old days" were not all that good. Besides that, we cannot go back, nor would we like to, even if it were possible. We are living in a new day and planning for a new future. This is no time for negativism, pessimism, or defeatism. May God lift our vision to higher heights as we plan for progress in His kingdom.

Chapter 19

THE SLEEPING SICKNESS OF STATUS QUOISM

Status quoism is the fatal philosophy which says, We are getting along just fine as we are. Our church is big enough but not too big. We are raising enough money to pay our bills and budgets and give our pastor a small salary increase every year or two. We don't have big revivals but now and then someone does get saved. We do lose members but also we take in a few now and then to patch up the losses. Although we are about the size we were 5, 10, 15, or 20 years ago, this is not an alarming situation to us, because the Methodists are not doing much either. Besides that, the country is in a big mess, Satan is running loose on every hand, and the community around our church is deteriorating. In other words, status quoism means maintaining things as they are.

This deadly disease comes on gradually (and at first imperceptibly) but eats like the deadly cancer that it is into the very vitals of the church, destroying faith, hope, and growth. This deadly stagnation causes a church to be less than a church and makes it become something of a high-class religious club or a society for sleeping saints. What are some of the self-defeating patterns which show up as indicators of this disease of status quoism? Let us examine a few.

1. *Failure-oriented preaching.* Immediately the question arises: Is it preaching at all if it is failure oriented? This is the kind of preaching that spends more time on the don'ts than on the do's for the Christian life, spreads more gloom and doom than faith and hope. It is the kind of preaching that assumes that the church ought not to grow; it is the kind of preaching that has the negative outlook and the pessimistic viewpoint. Often this preaching is declaiming, not exhorting, not spilling forth the Good News. And it sometimes takes the strange twist of raking the people over the coals for their lethargy and their lack of concern.

2. *Anemic administration.* This is the growth-equals-loss philosophy. It says in substance, Let's not plan too far ahead and let's not plan too big. This weak leadership is sometimes reflected in the pastor and sometimes reflected in the lives of those who are leaders in the church. It sets no challenging goals for new converts to be won or members to be received on profession of faith. It makes no plans for intense stewardship in areas of tithing, double-tithing, visitation, soul winning, or advance planning.

3. *Puny promotion.* This deadly philosophy is exactly opposite of that which was displayed on the Day of Pentecost and beyond, when the Early Church moved ahead with great strides. Their promotional philosophy was this: There is a whole world to win, and the Great Commission urges us onward. Status quoism says, Radio and television and the printed press have made the gospel available to everyone who is interested; therefore we will simply open our doors and let them come in if they are hungry enough.

4. *Brinkmanship financing.* This is the kind of financial planning which pays no attention to tithing campaigns or planned budgets or future building fund needs or

long-range planning for expansion or relocation. It is the kind of financing where the pastor and the church board are content to sit still with a hope-for-the-best attitude while the treasurer's report shows mounting deficits. It is the kind of financing which ignores the 10-month budget payment plans until six weeks before the district assembly. It is the kind of financing which wallows in its own inertia, expecting some gift from a wealthy person to bring them through the crisis. It is the short-ranged financing which has no large vision, which waits until the situation is on the brink of financial disaster and then begins a hand-wringing campaign which would not have been necessary at all if there had been alert leadership.

5. *Static organizational structure.* In this area, we see the absence of new blood coming into leadership. The same leaders which were in the saddle 5 years, 10 years, 20 years ago are still there and still using outdated methods and programming. The Sunday school superintendent is saying the same things in the so-called opening exercises that he said 10 and 20 years ago. The three or four who pray public prayers are praying with the same words that they used when they were first put in office. The missionary leaders are reading their way through their dull programs with no imagination and no innovation. The treasurer is still controlling the checkbook and perhaps refusing to write checks simply because he does not agree with the action of the board.

The pastor lets all of this slide by year after year because he himself is not in step with the times, is not in tune with what is happening around him. No new person has been elected to the church board for a number of years, and if elected to the church board, is not given a voice in the organizational leadership of the church. There is not a filling station, not a grocery store, not a bank in town that would dare to operate on such outdated methods as some churches are allowing.

6. *Insipid evangelism.* A low level of expectancy at revival time is a sure evidence of the sleeping sickness of status quoism. There is no advance planning and preparation. Few if any visitors or unconverted people are brought into the revival, and thus if anyone comes to the altar, it must be someone who has already been a professing Christian—which is fine except that the church's mission is broader than that.

7. *Sickness of rutism.* The church that makes no changes, that does not accept innovation, that does not open its doors to the fresh air of progress, is not likely to be able to even maintain the status quo for a very long period of time. Retrogression is sure to come. You either go forward or you slip back.

8. *The creeping paralysis of nonemotionalism.* When holiness church members begin to brag about their dignity and their quietness in their services, they cease to become holiness people. The joy of the Lord is our strength, and if this joy is present, it must bubble over on occasion!

9. *The death rattle of noninvolvement.* If there is a "Do Not Disturb" sign on the pastor's study door or on the Sunday school superintendent's desk, then the death dew has already settled on that church. One of the marks of truly spiritual people is that they are willing to be involved in the responsibilities of the church. If public appeals are necessary to locate teachers or others who will assume responsibility, then there is danger ahead.

Chapter 20

GAMES FAILURES PLAY

For some, failure does not seem to come easily. They have to work at it or make a game of it. At least they achieve it by conscious or unconscious effort and seem to enjoy games that failures play. Failure-prone people have two common denominators—self-deception and the abuse of time. All failures act as if they were going to live on earth 1,000 years. Most successful failures are not idlers; they are piddlers, dabblers, self-deceiving, undisciplined game players who salve a sorry conscience rather than strive for worthy goals.

In *Wake Up and Live,* Dorothea Brande reminds us that failure is "the intention, often unconscious, to fill life so full of secondary activities that there will be no time to perform the best works of which one is capable."[1] Someone else has said that some people seem to "pursue failure as a primary career." There are failures in the spiritual realm too. Some of them have been in the church a long time— not only failures personally, but also contributing to the failure of the church as a whole. Let us look at some of the games these failures play.

1. *The trivia game.* This game is played by people who avoid significant and worthwhile activities while they spend endless hours in work "invented" for themselves. They involve themselves in endless details which are of secondary value and leave the important things undone or done shabbily. They are piddlers—always busy at good little things while the world is on its way to destruction. Of them it could accurately be said, "Much ado about nothing."

2. *The charm game.* People playing this game have much personality appeal and many talents but produce little or nothing for God and the church. I was reminded of those who play this game as we passed by one of the windows in my wife's favorite department store. There he stood for all to see, dressed in his finest suit, neatest tie, sharpest shirt, and wearing shoes of the very latest design. He was the most charming-looking man you could ever wish to see. And he must have been a good Christian too, judging by his high standards, for this gentleman had never been to a filthy movie, had never smoked a cigarette, had never drunk liquor, had never been on a dance floor, and had never taken the name of God in vain. But sad to say, he had never been to church, he had never paid his tithe, he had made not one call on an absentee. Not once had he knocked on the door of a stranger and invited him to the house of God. You see, he was a manikin in the department store window. He was playing the Charm Game—one of the games that failures play.

3. *Obsession Game.* Players of this one are always intensely occupied with their favorite obsession. Some of them are pathological bookworms, reading every book as soon as it comes off the press. Some of them are crossword puzzle fans—always brushing up on the latest gimmicks in this area. Others can tell you the latest scores made by their favorite football, baseball, or basketball athletes. Still others know where the finest fishing and hunting is done. Others travel across the country to discover new

131

pleasures. But these Obsession players are grinding no grist for God. They cannot be nailed down to do God's work or harnessed to achieve Kingdom purposes.

4. *The Somnambulation Game.* Those who play this game sleep from one to four hours more each day than is necessary. Sometimes they spend an equal amount of time beyond this in bed, watching television, talking on the telephone, reading, or indulging in ease and pleasure. Often they are angered by interruptions. They are wearing themselves out with excessive head rest. But they are playing the game of failure by wasting all this time under false pretense. They are justifying what some people call pure laziness.

5. *The See-My-Scars Game.* Those who play this game declare that they are not able to produce in God's work because of childhood experiences which militate against them. Perhaps their parents or grandparents rejected them in infancy or childhood, leaving scars which keep them from being at their best in the church. Others have had unfortunate experiences in the loss of companions or children or parents which caused them to retreat into their shells. They nurse lifelong wounds and brag about the running sores in their personalities, likewise excusing themselves from spiritual endeavors in the kingdom of God. Others will complain that as children they were forced to go to church and therefore they refuse to go now. Some claim they have rejected God's will for their lives on the basis that their parents forced them to sit too long in family prayers when they were children.

6. *The Go-go Game.* These are the relentless partygoers who are so busy enjoying life that they do not have time for the work of the church. Often we see them on weekend trips, going to the mountains, the oceans, the lakes, but never to church. They don't attend church when the weather is nice because they are away on trips, but

132

they don't attend when the weather is bad either because they are afraid to expose themselves to the elements.

7. *The Hypochondria Game.* The players of this game enjoy poor health and drag around on Sundays and on Wednesday nights and especially during revival times, complaining of many pains that keep them out of church. They are always going to the doctor and yet the doctor is never able to find much wrong with them. It is interesting to compare them with successful people. Have you ever heard a successful man talk about his health? If he is sick, no one knows about it, and he talks about it only to the family doctor.

8. *The Irrelevant Game.* These are the people who deliberately undertake activities of relatively minor importance in the church—activities which they enjoy immensely and which are not time-consuming and which cost them nothing. Usually they are willing to display their talents before a large crowd but are unwilling to assume responsibilities of an obscure nature. They may spend long hours perfecting abilities in training so they may appear in public, but they will not turn a hand to knock on a door.

9. *The Alibi Game.* This one involves people who have an excuse for every failure, a reason why they have accomplished nothing in the church. They always have big plans for tomorrow, however. They promise to assume some responsibility within a matter of weeks or months but, alas, they never find time to fulfill the promise. They are always going to do great things for God next year, but next year never comes.

10. *The Talkathon Game.* These are the people who talk as if words were going out of style. Their telephones are always busy. They capture full attention at every party and are always gossiping over the back fence with their neighbors. These are the people who know all the answers to all the problems in the church. They are vocal about

their plan to make the church succeed, but are short on the effort needed to help it succeed.

This little bit of doggerel from the pen of some unknown author describes these people:

> *Some men die in the battle,*
> *Some men die in the flames,*
> *Some die inch by inch*
> *Playing little games.*

Chapter 21

TWELVE KEYS TO PROFICIENCY

In the first few chapters of the Book of Joshua we see standing out in bold relief a score of keys to proficiency that apply to laymen and ministers alike. If "success is achieving one's highest potential in his chosen field of service," then surely Joshua was a successful person. Let us examine twelve of these keys he used.

1. *Turn from the past.* "Moses . . . is dead" (1:2). God's announcement to Joshua was neither to inform him nor to console him. It was to make him quit the backward look to the good old days when Moses was alive, and make him look forward to even better days because God was still alive. People who look backward are not going forward. God's way to go forward is to profit from the past, not to live in it. He was saying to Joshua: Turn from your past heroes, your past successes, your past failures, and get on the road of progress to a better day!

2. *Know where you are going.* "Go over this Jordan . . . unto the land which I do give to them, even to the children of Israel" (1:2). Joshua saw it all as he waited in an awesome hour before God. And I think he trembled at the thrill of it, aware of his heavenly assignment. Blessed is the man who knows where he is going and how to get there. Blessed is the preacher and the church

board who know where the people ought to go and how to lead them there.

3. ***Think BIG.*** God does. "From the wilderness . . . even unto the great river . . . and unto the great sea" (1:4). One of the most perplexing problems church leaders face is this: "How can we get the people to make large plans?" We see so many tiny Sunday school rooms, so many small church buildings, so many puny plans, so many narrow-visioned saints . . . all in a big, wide world that is starving for the gospel we preach. Besides, we are backed up by all the resources of heaven!

4. ***Cultivate a sanctified self-esteem.*** "There shall not any man be able to stand before thee" (1:5). This is not the unholy egotism of a bluffing bigot. It is God's promised presence in the life of His yielded servant. It is not based on a holier-than-thou brand of super-spirituality. It is the sanctified self-image which God's holy achievers always have when they know they are in the center of the will of God. Are you a child of the King? Then believe it and demonstrate it! With Paul you can say, "I can do all things through Christ which strengtheneth me" (Phil. 4:13). Your motto will be that of the martyred missionary Jim Elliot, who said: "Find God's will and live it to the hilt."

5. ***Stand on bedrock.*** "I will be with thee: I will not fail thee, nor forsake thee" (1:5). What better foundation could any leader find? There is no shifting sand beneath his feet, for God's Word cannot fail. Promises like this come in mighty handy when plans backfire and controversy arises and opposition strikes terror to the trembling heart. Do you know what it is to take your burdens to the place of prayer and agonize until some personal promise for that moment flashes out from God's Word and gives you a sure footing? This is one of the indispensable keys to adequacy in God's work.

6. ***Develop a robust backbone.*** "Be strong and of a

good courage" (1:6). Joshua needed to hear that, for the sting of a former setback for which he was not responsible was still smarting. God knew that, from a human standpoint, Joshua faced an impossible task. So three times in four verses God said it to Joshua: Be brave, be bold, be firm, be fearless, be gallant, be heroic, be determined, be dauntless; show your mettle, your pluck; shun fear, shun cowardice, refuse to be discouraged! Every man can discipline his moods. And the successful man does just that.

7. *Play by the rules.* "Do according to all the law . . . turn not from it" (1:7). There are four sets of rules every churchman must follow in God's work: *(a)* the Bible, *(b)* the church *Manual, (c)* parliamentary procedure, and *(d)* conscience. If the rules in any of these four areas are bypassed, there is trouble ahead. I knew a pastor who did not strictly adhere to the rules applying to the conduct of some church business. Someone challenged him and there was no way to defend what had been done. Confusion and opposition arose. I knew a church which ignored a building code of the city (and bypassed the instructions of the Church Extension Board) and consequently suffered many entanglements and considerable expense. If it is important for athletes to play by the rules, how much more important is it for church leaders!

8. *Learn to delegate responsibility.* "Command the people" (1:11). Delegating is not easy for some leaders, for they think it is easier to do it themselves (to be sure it is done right) than to get someone else to do it. But this is fallacious thinking. One person can do only a given amount of work and do it well. If he allows himself to be saddled with more than he can do, he is showing a weakness in his leadership. Of course it is not easy to get competent workers in the church—but it is very necessary to get and/or train the best possible. People *can* be motivated

and challenged to accept responsibilities. And they must be! It is a basic part of true leadership.

9. *Organize for effectiveness.* "Prepare . . . for within three days ye shall pass over this Jordan" (1:11). Think of all the preparation and organization that went with moving 1 million or so people into new territory— enemy territory, if you please! There were tents and clothes and babies and old folk and cattle and all sorts of other possessions which had to be packed up and moved across the Jordan—and without professional movers and moving vans! And only three days' notice! Joshua learned in a hurry that organization was important. And he did it right the first time! Is your household well organized? Look around and see for yourself. Glance around your study or office and see how well organized you are. A five-minute glance at your church and its records will provide ample indication of the efficiency of its leaders.

10. *Create a climate of high morale.* "All that thou commandest us we will do, and whithersoever thou sendest us, we will go" (1:16). I like that kind of response. It is the extreme opposite of the response of nearly 40 years before when they were first challenged to enter the Promised Land. Then they were about to stone their leaders; now they were eager with anticipation. How can we explain the change? Morale! It was time to get out of the wilderness and Joshua had struck the spark which made them feel they could go in and possess the land.

11. *Calculate the risks.* "Go view the land" (2:1). Two spies were sent out to look things over and report their findings to Joshua. He wanted to know what to expect over on the west bank. The wise leader is never caught off guard. He plans for every eventuality because he antici- pates. When men dig tunnels through mountains, they know where they are coming out. Jesus spoke about mili- tary men who, before they engaged in battle, calculated

the risks to see whether they could win. I have sat with leading laymen as we calculated the risks of an anticipated building program. How much would it cost? How much could we raise? How much would we need to borrow? How much could we afford to borrow? How could we sell this venture to our people? How many people would we lose (and how much money would we lose) by this relocation? What would happen if we failed to relocate at this time?

12. *Get your feet wet.* "The feet of the priests . . . were dipped in the brim of the water" (3:15). Joshua got something going! They did not stand and dread the water, nor test it with the toe. They got their feet wet—they marched right in! It is said that Genghis Khan, the Asiatic conqueror, had a special strategy: He marched straight for the enemy and threw everything he had at them. It is time to abandon useless and meaningless activities and engage in the action that produces growth and progress. Get your feet wet—get going!

Alexis Carrel, noted scientist, wrote these exciting lines:

> Nature . . . favors those who are sober, alert, intelligent and enthusiastic; most of all, those who have the courage to take the risks and who possess the will to succeed. She smiles on those who are ready to live hard and dangerously.[1]

Chapter 22

BROTHER HO-HUM
COMES ALIVE

We have been considering the "grasshopper complex" —what the evidences of it are and how it operates in the lives of people. It is time now to observe what can be done about negative attitudes and the defeatism of failure. How can we change "grasshoppers" into giants?

At the outset, we must realize that failure is the result of the wrong kind of habits. Contrariwise, achievement is the result of certain disciplined habits. Therefore, if we are to see old Brother Ho-hum or Sister Easygoing come alive, we must change their habits of thinking and their approach to life in general. This is not easily done, nor will everyone respond to our suggestions, but it is well worth the effort, for all it takes is a few inspired people to make a church come alive.

1. *Eliminate the deadly de-motivators that cripple people.* I suggest four of these—doubt, fear, the past, and the future.

Some say, "It can't be done." Nothing so demoralizes the saints as when these words are spoken in a board meeting. When a fellow says it can't be done, he does not often have a good explanation for making such a statement. If you ask him why, he will often say, "We never did it that

140

way before," or, "It is too big a job for this size of congregation."

The second deadly de-motivator that must be eliminated is fear. The usual wording is "I am afraid that . . ." Usually they say it costs too much, we do not have time, nobody will support it, people are not interested in it, etc. Doubt and fear are deadly de-motivators of the church and of the human personality.

The third of these is the past. Often people express this by saying, "I have been a failure all my life; I can never do anything right." "I tried it and it wouldn't work." "Nobody likes me; I am not rich, I'm not handsome, I do not have a pleasing personality; therefore, I am a flop." The ghosts of the past often ride right into our board meetings and into our congregational meetings to demoralize our people.

The fourth deadly de-motivator that must be eliminated is the future. "What if . . . ?" "What if it doesn't work?" "What if we do not get the money?" "What if nobody will support it?" "What if the project fails?" And on and on. The list is endless. People are afraid to venture because they are afraid of the future. Basically they are afraid of themselves.

How can we eliminate these deadly de-motivators? All of these are condemned by Jesus and by the writers of the Gospels and the Epistles. Preachers sometimes tell people that these problem areas of doubt and fear and the past and the future are all taken care of in full consecration at an altar of prayer. This is true spiritually, but many good people live constantly with doubt and fear and with problems of the past and future. They have yet to learn the deep lessons of faith and trust for everyday needs. The Scriptures show how these deadly de-motivators can be overcome and life can be well rounded and useful.

2. *Take on the faith formula of Jesus.* Few things

are as exciting as the faith that Jesus demonstrated and promised. This was the faith that motivated the Early Church as well. The thrilling words of our Lord were a part of their everyday life: "If ye abide in me, and my words abide in you, ye shall ask what ye will, and it shall be done unto you." Again He said, "What things soever ye desire, when ye pray, believe that ye receive them, and ye shall have them." He also said, "With God all things are possible." And again, "Nothing shall be impossible unto you." One of the problems we moderns face is that we try to explain these promises away, but the Early Church did not have that problem. Instead of explaining away these truths, they embraced them and made them a part of their everyday living.

Are these promises of our Lord true or are they false? Is there such a thing as "achieving faith," or is this only a mistaken idea that we picked up somewhere? If we want people to come alive in our churches, the best gift we can give them is the gift of faith promised by our Lord. Once a man gets a glimpse of truth, it will be difficult to put him to sleep. He will be so excited that he will want to have a part in the great accomplishments that always come through faith.

3. *Cultivate attitudes that motivate.* We must not only get into the habit of doubting our doubts and believing our beliefs, but we must also develop those attitudes that motivate us and motivate others.

I pastored two people in the same church some years ago and was amazed at their contrasting personalities. One of these was a very fine Christian woman but her outlook on life was purely negative. When I said to her, "It is a beautiful day," she would reply, "Yes, but it's going to rain tomorrow." When I commented, "We had a good service last Sunday, didn't we?" she would reply, "Yes, but the old devil is going to get us if we don't watch out." When

I asked, "How do you feel today?" she said, "I feel fairly tolerable today, but I'll be down again by tomorrow." Her attitudes were thoroughly demoralizing, even in the church and in the Sunday school class which she attended. Her testimonies left people defeated and discouraged rather than inspired.

In this same church was a man who was president of the men's Sunday school class. He was faithful in his attendance, always arriving early, always standing at the door and shaking hands with people. He always greeted people with a broad smile and a firm handclasp and a pat on the shoulder and a remark about how wonderful it is to be alive. Many new men came to the Sunday school class just because they liked to be with Bill.

What was the difference in these two people? The difference was in their attitudes. One had an attitude that motivated himself and inspired others; the other had an attitude that demoralized. With a little determination, anyone can improve his way of thinking and change his habit patterns as well as his words and actions. The fellow who never gets excited about anything needs to be challenged to get excited about the greatest thing in the world —living the Christian life.

4. *Begin believing like a winner.* All of us know people who believe and think like losers. They always magnify the fact that the church is backslidden, that the world is going to the dogs, people do not care about religion, that the modern home is disintegrating, that the Communists are about to overtake us, and there is no hope in sight for the future.

But all of us are acquainted, too, with people who believe and think like winners. I know a pastor who took over the leadership of a small, defeated, discouraged congregation. They had no money, their property was thoroughly inadequate, they could not pay their budgets, they were downcast, they were at the bottom from every standpoint. The new pastor came in with joy and radiance in his eyes, his conversation, and in his preaching. He ignored their defeatism and began to brag on what Jesus had already done for him and was going to do for them. He told them they could double their attendance, they could pay off all their debts, they could sell the old parsonage, they could build a new church, they could pay their budgets, they could triple their income, and they could become one of the strongest churches on the district.

Of course they didn't believe it at first, but he kept telling them this and kept preaching faith and joy and courage and hope and love and victory and cleansing and power until people began to loosen up and get blessed and say, "Amen." New people began to attend and ended up at the altar. It wasn't long before that pastor was taking in more new members than any other church on the district. He won all the awards that could be offered the very first year. The second year he broke all previous records and started a building program. They moved their old parsonage away and built a new sanctuary in its place. Today that church is still on the rise.

It all happened because one man began to live and believe like a winner and preach like a winner. This was the kind of preaching Jesus did. This was the kind of preaching Paul did. This is the kind of preaching that gets results today. Therefore, if people are to come alive in the service of the Master, they must be awakened by someone who is already alive, alert, aware, full of faith, motivated to carry the gospel across the world.

I believe that in every church, no matter how small, there is at least one man who could set that congregation on fire if he would make up his mind to do so with God's help. He can do this by mastering his moods, by getting excited about living, by looking on the bright side of life,

144

by accepting faith as a new way of life, by the practice of appreciation and gratitude in all that he does.

Instead of scolding people for their lack of involvement or knocking them because of their excuses, let's get excited ourselves and keep ourselves motivated. Then we will be able to convince the detractors of the scriptural possibilities of faith. Always be bragging on one another, always be bragging on Jesus, and always be pointing the "unbelievers" to greater things ahead.

This means that we must make every day and every service in the church a delight. It means that every contact we make with our people, on the street, in the home, in the church, in the hospital, must be radiant and optimistic and must have in it the essence of hope and the anticipation of a better tomorrow. It is time for every Brother Ho-hum to come alive. The love of Christ constrains us to come alive. The call of Christ compels us to come alive. Our consecration says to us that we must come alive. World conditions stab us awake and command us to be a church alive. The soon coming of Christ insists that we be alive to meet Him in the air!

Chapter 23

HOW TO SUSTAIN MOTIVATION

Have you ever noticed that undisciplined people can get all worked up and enthusiastic, but after a little while they are back in the rut of negativism with the attitude of failure again? Why is this? And how can we overcome this problem in the church? What can we do to sustain this motivation, both in the leadership and in the congregation in our churches?

It has been observed that true leadership exists only where there is ability to generate morale. Perhaps we should add that effective leadership always finds a way to persist in the area of morale and motivation. The pastor himself must know what it takes to achieve and excel. So must key leaders in the church catch this insight.

Success always depends more on motivation than on methods. The ancient Demosthenes said to his rival orator, Aeschines, "You make them say, 'How well he speaks'; I make them say, 'Let's march against Philip.'" Action is imperative, but action must have a sustained follow-through if success is to be won and maintained.

If the leader does not lead, another will arise to take his place. This is a law that applies to individuals, to local churches, and to denominations. Let us then consider here some suggestions geared to help us maintain persistent motivation on the part of both the pastor and the congregation.

1. *Maintain constant spiritual and mental renewal.* Perhaps nothing else is as important as this. Most people and most programs bog down because of a lack of either mental or spiritual renewal or both. This involves daily prayer—not just saying prayers but praying through. It consists of being "on top" spiritually. This means constantly living the Spirit-filled life, reinforcing and reaffirming one's call to God's service, and locating fresh promises daily in God's Word. It means mastering the art of self-discipline in areas of time, money, devotional life, and Christian service. It involves filling one's personality with zest, spice, love for living, and love for people. To do this, there must be a constant reevaluation to see where we stand. Have we slipped? Where have we failed? There must be a renewed determination never to allow discouragement, defeat, or negativism to possess us. As Paul put it, there must be a "renewing of your mind."

2. *Stay on top of your attitudes.* The man who is to exercise a persistent motivational leadership must constantly sharpen his attitudes and disciplines. This means that he will eliminate factors which could limit his progress, such as destructive thoughts which might creep into his mind. He will maintain a "child of the King" concept about himself. This sanctified self-confidence is not a carnal holier-than-thou attitude. Rather it is a humble yet challenging self-concept which enables a man to stand tall in the face of his own problems and challenges.

The constant demand these days is for achievement-oriented thoughts. But this is not out of harmony with the very sound teachings of Jesus and others. "As [a man] . . . thinketh in his heart, so is he," is more than a sage saying. It is eternal scripture from God's Word which applies to us today.

147

Also, there is the discipline of desire. To stay on top of one's attitudes means that one will not allow his desires to lead him astray or to take him down the wrong trails. And again, if one is to stay on top of his attitudes, he is obliged to maintain a high level of enthusiasm in his own personal mind and heart at all times.

3. *Upgrade your priorities.* The man who does not set himself goals—immediate, intermediate, and long-range—is himself lacking in leadership qualities. The leader who would maintain a high-level thrust of motivation in himself and in his people is one who makes planning a vital part of his living. He pays attention to programming for himself and for his people.

I recall some teens who said to their pastor as they decided to stop coming to church, "You don't have anything going to keep us interested." How tragic it is that anything as appealing as the gospel and any organization as worthy as a church has not found a way to program something that will have a vital impact on the lives of teen-agers. We must come to grips with the needs of the people, rather than adopt a "head-in-the-sand" approach. This means staying on top of the financial situation and spiritual effort as well. It means that objectives must not only be established but often revised and upgraded.

This involves the very best of communication, that people not only may understand each other but may be kept informed of what is ahead. Our goal setting must be done by people who are involved in reaching the goals rather than by having goals imposed upon them from the organizational structure above.

4. *Place positive people in leadership.* If there is to be persistent motivation, there must be positive-thinking people in leadership in the church. This includes not only the pastor but the key people within the organization of the church. Those who scoff and say that there isn't anything

to the idea of positive thoughts have forgotten that God's Word says, "Whatsoever things are pure, whatsoever things are lovely, whatsoever things are of good report . . . think on these things" (Phil. 4:8).

Pessimistic leaders who stand and whine in the presence of the people or silently sow seeds of negativism cannot in any way sustain a spiritual thrust in the church. Rather they are a hindrance to it. This may necessitate a change in leadership personnel on occasion. Of course, the ideal is to change the people from being negative to optimistic thinkers. But if they do not change, if they persist in their pessimistic thinking, it is better to place someone else in leadership who has optimism, courage, and faith that God's work can be accomplished.

5. *Don't dictate; demonstrate.* The best way to accomplish this is to be sure that a relaxed atmosphere prevails in the meetings. Encourage people to be creative in their thinking and in their planning. If people are relaxed and creative, they will work better together and they will also be more loyal to their leader than if the leader himself is a dictator. This is not a plea for weak or anemic leadership. It is only a suggestion that the best kind of leadership is that which involves responsible people in decision making and goal setting. How wonderful it is to see a strong dynamism throughout an organization, where everyone is pulling together, loving each other, working toward a common goal.

6. *Delegate; don't do it all yourself.* You will recall the illustration given earlier of how Moses tried to do it all himself while the people stood around all day with nothing to do. Then came Jethro, his father-in-law, who showed him the fallacy of his operation and suggested that he take another approach and involve the people. So Moses delegated the work that he was doing into the hands of responsible leadership. As a consequence, Moses was able to do

better work than he had been doing previously, and he also trained other leaders to work alongside of him. It is doubtful that Moses would have lived to be 120 if he had tried to do everything by himself all those years.

7. *Encourage dialog and response.* Let people talk back without being put on the spot. A good way to do this is occasionally to pass out evaluation sheets and ask the people to give their opinions in certain areas, or perhaps in any area. Have them turn in the sheets unsigned. If this can be supplemented with discussion, so much the better. A leader needs this feedback in order to know if he is on the right track and if what he is doing is being received and accepted by those who are participating with him.

Sometimes a suggestion box is a good way to get evaluation from the people. Again, at times, a straw ballot can be taken without any official motion or second being offered. Simply let the people express a yes or no to the proposition before them without having to sign their names or without having to make a legal pronouncement on the question at hand.

Such evaluation is imperative for leadership. A leader needs to keep his hand on the pulse of the people. People will not always be frank enough to tell a man to his face that they disagree with his policies, but if given an opportunity they may do so anonymously. This evaluation not only helps the leader but it assists those working with him. It helps to keep morale and motivation at a high level at all times because the people know they can express themselves without recrimination.

8. *Keep the spiritual fires burning at all times.* There can be no substitute for the spiritual flame in the hearts of leaders, both lay and ministerial, in the local church. Let the pastor keep his people on their knees. Let him preach so that they will keep blessed in their hearts.

Let him challenge them so that they will recognize the seriousness of their responsibility.

Above all, let the preacher and other leaders keep their own hearts melted and blessed at all times. If there are apologies to be made, they should be made quickly. If there are broken friendships, they should be mended immediately. If there are barriers, they must be broken down without delay. In the Early Church, those who were filled with the Holy Spirit on the Day of Pentecost were again and again filled with the Holy Spirit beyond Pentecost. God's plan calls for us not only to be saved and sanctified but to keep Spirit-filled and fire-baptized at all times.

Chapter 24

PREPARING YOURSELF FOR ACTION

Many church leaders would like very much to advance their church but have not learned the techniques for sustaining progress. Here are some suggestions that could apply to pastors or to lay leaders alike in their quest for progress either in areas of building programs, tithing campaigns, fund-raising campaigns, Sunday school contests, attendance drives, or even revivals. These principles are not in the form of a specific, detailed plan for a given program but are the background approaches and basics for moving any program ahead.

1. *Believe in yourself, in God, and in your task.* Faith is the beginning point for any achievement. You must believe in what you are doing and believe in the One who can help you. God believes in you or you would not be where you are today. Your church believes in you and has given you your assignment. Therefore, you must believe in yourself, in your work, in your church, in your future, in your people, and in God who can help you.

2. *Kill the rattlesnake of discouragement.* This means you will need to master your moods, control your emotions, and use faith-lifting scriptures for your daily mottoes. If you think it cannot be done, it cannot—at least

by you. If you believe you can do the assignment, there is no doubt you can do it. "According to your faith be it unto you." Discouraged people never get anything going.

3. *Flex those muscles of morale.* Build a team spirit. Talk like an achiever. Live on tiptoe. Let your enthusiasm show through. Be your own self-starter. Let your enthusiasm bubble over to motivate other people. Do not be afraid of contests, campaigns, excitement, promotion, awards, goals, and all the other things that it takes to make God's work go.

4. *Establish confidence.* By this we mean the leader must gain respect for his leadership. Confidence in leadership cannot be bestowed. It is not automatic; it must be earned. And it starts with a leader who has confidence in himself. If he exudes confidence, he can replace doubt with trust among his people. He can replace conflict with unity. To gain confidence on the part of others for yourself as a leader, you must act decisively and positively, yet impartially and lovingly. Create an air of expectancy. Unite faith and action in the minds of the people. Involve your people in decisions which affect them and in goals which they themselves must reach.

5. *Arm yourself with all the facts.* You should know all there is to know about your situation. You should dig below the surface and get an in-depth concept of what you are doing and how the people are thinking. Always get to the root of the problem at hand before you try to deal with it. Knowledge of all the facts will increase the confidence people can place in you and give you greater insight and faith in your work. These facts should be made known to the people so that they will know, too, what is happening, what has happened, and what is about to happen.

6. *Know where you are going and how to get there.* Have some goals for yourself rather than stumble in the dark. People pay attention to the man who knows where he is going. What are your immediate goals for a particular situation? What are your intermediate goals for next matter of weeks or months? What are your long-range goals over a period of years?

7. *Know where your people ought to go and how to lead them there.* Be a leader, for you fill a leader's shoes. God's leaders have been men who could lead, not men who drive. Therefore, work with your people in setting their goals. Do not impose your goals but enable them to establish their own, even if they are different from yours.

8. *Calculate the risks involved.* This means you will look ahead! Know how you plan to accomplish your goals. There will be risks involved which you must calculate. Leaders face many forks in the road. Their choices sometimes have drastic consequences, which proves that foresight is more necessary than hindsight. Jesus indicated that a general would be foolish to take his men into battle against a stronger army without knowing the strength of both. So know your resources but be willing to venture.

Chapter 25

PREPARING YOUR PEOPLE FOR ACTION

If your church is one of those with a gloomy, defeatist, pessimistic outlook on life, you can light a candle, and I challenge you to do it, whether you are a minister or a layman. It is your church, it is your responsibility, it is your opportunity. Here are some ways to "turn the people on."

1. *Change the way your people think.* If they are thinking small, help them to think big. If they are thinking failure, help them to think success. If they are thinking defeat, help them to think victory. If they are living in the past, help them live in the present and look to the future. To change the way they think, you will have to give them an abundance of scriptures from God's Word and practical illustrations of how God is blessing in other churches. Above all, give them yourself—full of faith and victory.

2. *Give them something better than what they have.* They have fears; give them faith. They have despair; give them hope. They have doubt; give them confidence. If the church is not growing, show them that it can grow. If the revivals have not been accomplishing much, show them how they can be made successful. If the building needs to be improved, show them how it can be changed. If there is not enough money raised, show them

how they can increase income. If the church needs to be relocated, show them how and even where they can move. Jesus always gave people something better than what they had, and He expects His followers to do the same.

3. *Lift their self-esteem.* It may be that they do not think too well of themselves. They may consider themselves grasshoppers but in reality God wants them to consider themselves to be giants. They may look upon themselves as doomed, but God wants them to look upon themselves as victors. Enable them to see that they are stamped with the image of the King and have all of the qualities that are necessary for an achieving church if they will develop them.

4. *Be a morale builder in the church.* Have you ever observed how an awkward child can walk through a room one time and leave in his trail mussed-up furniture, rumpled rugs, twisted lamps, knocked-over books, and crooked pictures? We smile and say that such a person is in the "awkward stage" of his life. The dreadful part about it is that some people stay in this stage of life even when they have lived a long time, especially in matters that relate to morale and motivation. I have observed people on board meetings, who, with a few choice sentences, could do more to demoralize people and leave the entire program in a shambles and do it quicker than almost anyone would believe possible. But while there are a few people like this, there are within each of us potentialities for morale building. By a little self-discipline, study, meditation, prayer, and Bible reading, it is possible for a person to turn around a church board that is headed in the wrong direction. He can give them courage, hope, confidence, assurance, and strength for tomorrow.

5. *Show them how to dream.* Some people have never learned to visualize, to project, to anticipate. They have no goals for tomorrow or six months away or six years

away. Likewise some church boards have no definite plans for the future. They operate day by day, month by month, year by year, with scarcely ever a thought of planning ahead and dreaming. You may be the person to show your church how to dream dreams, how to look ahead, how to set goals, how to erect targets to shoot at. You may be the one to plan *with* your people (not *for* them) a set of challenging goals. Make it a cooperative project, for goals that are imposed from above do not have the involvement factor that produces motivation. Show your people how to dream.

6. *Gear up for growth.* Make plans for expansion. Expect to grow. Enlarge your organization for growth. Pay attention to the administrative areas that will open the doors to growth. This may mean organizing two classes where you now have one. It may mean asking other people to be teachers who are not now teaching. It may mean spending money to build extra Sunday school rooms so that there will be space for growth. Growth is not likely to come unless we plan for it, work for it, and make room for it. So let's get ready for it!

7. *Put some overalls on your people and lead them in old-fashioned hard work.* This means that people will respond to leadership. If you want to see work done, start working yourself and give somebody else a paintbrush to work along with you. Things will begin to move! Perhaps teen-agers and young adults will respond quicker than most anyone in this area and undoubtedly will be benefited more by having done the work themselves. Nothing lifts morale so much as working together for a common cause, especially when it is a labor of love. People will respond to a challenge but they are slow to take orders. They will respond better if the leader is setting the example in getting his hands dirty.

8. *Keep the altar fires burning.* If you are the pastor, this is your prime business. If you are not the pastor, you certainly can make it your prime business and encourage the pastor and encourage the people in this vital area. Defeated congregations are often inspired and lifted when everyone comes to the altar at the close of a service and prays until victory comes. People need to be challenged to pray through.

They also need to be challenged to fast and pray according to the scriptural pattern. Many of us can remember when fasting and prayer seemed to be the only hope when we needed a spiritual breakthrough. We would pray and fast for days until victory came. How glorious that victory was! God is still alive today, and His challenge is upon you and everyone in your congregation to light a candle of spiritual faith and achievement.

Reference Notes

PART ONE

Chapter 1:

1. Quoted by Laurence J. Peter in *The Peter Prescription* (New York: William Morrow Co., Inc., 1972), p. 207.

2. Elmer G. Leterman, *The Sale Begins when the Customer Says "No"* (New York: MacFadden-Bartell Corp., 1953), p. 185.

3. Lawrence Welk, *Guidelines for Successful Living* (New York: The New American Library, Inc., 1969), p. 116.

4. Catherine Marshall, *The Prayers of Peter Marshall* (Carmel, N.Y.: Guideposts Associates, Inc., 1954), p. 208.

Chapter 3:

1. Quoted by J. Oswald Sanders in *Spiritual Leadership* (Chicago: Moody Press, 1967), p. 22.

2. Dorothea S. Kopplin, *Something to Live By* (Garden City, N.Y.: Doubleday and Co., Inc., 1945), p. 146.

Chapter 4:

1. Dorothea Brande, *Wake Up and Live* (New York: Simon and Schuster, 1936), p. 83.

2. U. S. Andersen, *Success-Cybernetics* (West Nyack, N.Y.: Parker Publishing Co., Inc., 1966), p. 71.

3. *Ibid.,* p. 59.

Chapter 5:

1. Laurence J. Peter, *The Peter Principle* (New York: William Morrow Co., Inc., 1969), p. 121.

2. Vernon Howard, *Action Power* (Englewood Cliffs, N.J.: Prentice Hall, Inc., 1963), p. 46.

3. Quoted by Frederick Ellsworth Wolf, *Leadership in the New Age* (Boston: New Age Publications, 1937), p. 80.

Chapter 6:

1. Walter Guzzardi, Jr., *The Young Executives* (New York: The New American Library, Inc., 1964), p. 35.

2. Johnny Jernigan and Margaret Jernigan Ramsey, *Courageous Jernigan* (Kansas City: Nazarene Publishing House, 1974), p. 44.

3. William MacDonald, *True Discipleship* (Oak Park, Ill.: Midwest Christian Publishers, 1962), p. 27.

Chapter 7:

1. Joseph D. Cooper, *The Art of Decision Making* (Garden City, N.Y.: Doubleday and Co., 1961).

2. Stanton Vaughn, *700 Limerick Lyrics* (New York: Carey-Stafford Co., 1906), p. 157.

Chapter 8:

1. Donald A. Laird and Eleanor C. Laird, *The Techniques of Delegating* (New York: McGraw-Hill Book Co., Inc., 1957), p. 80.

PART TWO

Chapter 12:

1. Peter Drucker, *The Practice of Management* (New York: Harper and Brothers Publishers, 1954), p. 159.

PART THREE

Chapter 20:

1. Dorothea Brande, *Wake Up and Live* (New York: Simon and Schuster, 1936), p. 45.

Chapter 21:

1. Alexis Carrel, *Reflections on Life* (New York: Hawthorne Books, Inc., 1952).